IN THE SPIRIT OF PENTECOST

DEDICATION

To Sister Mary Augustine Cahill
together with the late Sisters Mary Mercy Brady
and Francis Mattimoe, and my eight companions
whom they nurtured in the Congregation of The Sisters of Mercy,
and who now minister joyfully to God's people in witness and
proclamation: Sisters Liamie Cummins, Sarah McDonald,
Patricia McMahon, Kathleen Doyle, Baptist Larke,
Anna Burke, Bridget Culhane and Majella Sheridan.

KATHLEEN M. MURPHY

In the Spirit of Pentecost

ST PAULS

All biblical quotations taken from the Revised Standard Version
(Catholic edition), Version 5, 1996 Christian Technologies, PO Box
2201, Independence MO 64055. Available on CD by the Division of
Christian Education, National Council for Churches in Christ, USA.

ST PAULS Publishing
187 Battersea Bridge Road, London SW11 3AS, UK
www.stpaulspublishing.com

ISBN 978-0-85439-749-5

Set by TuKan DTP, Fareham, UK
Printed by Melita Press, Malta

ST PAULS is an activity of the priests and brothers
of the Society of St Paul who proclaim the Gospel
through the media of social communication

ACKNOWLEDGEMENTS

Writing this book has been one of the great pleasures of my life to date because it has been requested by so many women and men who enjoyed and felt spiritually refreshed by its predecessor *The Women of the Passion* (2005). These people know who they are and I now offer my heartfelt gratitude and prayers to each one of them for challenging me afresh.

I extend my warmest appreciation and sincere thanks to my preliminary proof readers: Theresa Cowe who is one of our precious Glasgow Mercy Associates and Manager of Practice Learning, Glasgow School of Social Work at the University of Strathclyde, and Rosemarie O'Keeffe in Amble.

I am indebted in a special way to my Congregational Leader, Sister Philomena Bowers, for her very helpful observations on the final manuscript; and to Isabel Smyth SND, for making time to write a very thoughtful and helpful Foreword to this book despite her busy schedule. Isabel holds a Post Graduate Masters Degree in Women and Religion from Lancaster University. Currently she is the Catholic Bishops Associate Secretary for Inter Faith Relations and the convener of the Churches Agency for Inter Faith Relations in Scotland, a lecturer in the Centre for Inter Faith Studies at Glasgow University as well as a director of the Centre for Inter Faith and Spirituality in Bridge of Allan, Stirling.

Very special thanks are due to the Reverend Margaret Forrester of the Church of Scotland for reading the manuscript, discussing it with me and for her very generous and sisterly comment which can be read on the cover. As one of the first women to be ordained in her Church, Margaret has made a unique contribution to securing equality for women in ministry and to supporting and protecting their rights and dignity at all levels in society. Like Mary of Nazareth, and Catherine McAuley, the Venerable Foundress of my Religious Congregation, the Sisters of Mercy, Margaret has been a true pioneer and I am privileged to know her.

My heartfelt thanks are extended to Sisters Annette McCartan, Liamie Cummins, Moira Keane, Dominic Timmins, Perpetua McGrath, Evelyn Gallagher, Ita Keane Ninian Duffner, and Rose Marie Sheridan; to so many members of our Mercy Family, as well as to my sister Madge Nevills, her daughter Irene, my nephew James Murphy; to the Vallely family; and my many associates in ministry for their interest, gentle encouragement and affirming words.

I am deeply indebted to Sister Marie Henderson of our Detroit community for her artistic interpretation of my theme in the beautiful contemporary illustration which adds so much to the cover of this work. Marie, thank you very much indeed.

Finally, I offer my sincere thanks to Fr Andrew Pudussery SSP, recently retired Director of Publishing at St Pauls, to his successor Fr Celso Godilano and to Ms Annabel Robson, the Commissioning Editor at St Pauls for her thoughtful comments, advice, attention to detail and overall presentation in taking the material forward for publication. Annabel, you have been an inspiration.

Kathleen M Murphy
Feast of Our Lady of Mercy, 24 September 2008

Contents

Foreword   9

Introduction   11

Mary: A Model and an Inspiration
for All Ages and Cultures   15

Mary: Mother, Post Pentecost Pioneer
and Partner in Mission   34

Dorcas: Distinguished Disciple, Daughter
and Diplomat   54

Mary the Mother of John Mark: Protector,
Provider and Proclaimer   74

Lydia: Convert, Communicator and
Collaborator   93

Sapphira: Straying from the Spirit
and Settling with Satan   112

Euodia and Syntyche: Faith, Friendship,
Fragility and Fidelity   128

Lois and Eunice: Grandmother, Mother
and Mentor   146

Priscilla: Listener, Learner and Leader   166

Phoebe: Deacon, Daughter
and Delegate   189

Conclusion   207

Foreword

When I first discovered that there were no stories of women in the obligatory lectionary readings for Sundays I was not just taken aback that the women were absent but that I hadn't even noticed the omission. Nor did others when I mentioned it to them and this included priests and seminarians who would have to preach on these readings.

Feminist theologians and scripture scholars have taught us in recent years to read scripture 'against the grain' and to read behind the lines to discover the reality of the lives of women who are often mentioned only in passing. Sister Kathleen Murphy does just this with the lives of a number of the prominent women in the burgeoning Christian community and the early Church. By looking behind the text we are taken into the life of that early community in a way that makes it come to life. We can smell, hear and see the realities of that life with its struggles, its tensions, its joys and enthusiasms. We know of the work of people like Paul and Timothy but in this book we learn about women who managed businesses and households, who were respected in wider society as well as within their families. But above all, these were women who played a significant part in the early Christian community as leaders, evangelisers and perhaps even presiders at the community meal, the Eucharist. These were women whom Paul was not afraid to call friends, sisters, deacons, helpers, women who had the responsibility of sustaining and leading the new communities and who generously used their homes, their talents and their gifts in the service of the gospel, a gospel which Paul felt was safe in their hands. When we look carefully at the texts in Acts and Paul it becomes obvious how important these women were to the growth of the community, what a public role they played and yet we know so little of them. It is right and fitting that this book should reverse that situation.

The women mentioned in this book, however, are not just giants for their own day. In the reflection section of each chapter and in the prayers that conclude the chapters their relevance for today is clearly brought out. Readers are challenged to reflect on their lives in a way that connects with contemporary issues and to consider questions which challenge us in our ordinary daily life as well as in our membership of the Church at both local and universal level.

It must surely be in the spirit of Pentecost that this book uncovers and reveals the important contribution that women made to the early Church as it must surely be in the spirit of Pentecost that the contemporary Church recovers and acknowledges the great contribution of women who throughout the ages have played important but often hidden roles within the community. This book is a valuable contribution to this on-going task.

Isabel Smyth
Catholic Bishops' Associate Secretary for Inter Faith Relations
and Governor of the Churches' Agency for
Inter Faith Relations in Scotland

Introduction

When listening to, and reflecting on Sacred Scripture today, many women do so in the hope of finding inspiration for their own lives from stories of their foremother in faith and ministry. Frequently they are disappointed. There are a variety of reasons for this: apart from Mary the Mother of Jesus and Mary Magdalene, women in Scripture were never portrayed as active in witness and proclamation; the andro-centric writers of the New Testament concentrated on demonstrating how men transmitted the Good News; and homilists today, rarely consider the giftedness of the faith-filled women in *The Acts of the Apostles* and *The Letters of Paul.*

The only Scripture passages pertaining to women included in our liturgical cycles are those relating to Dorcas, Lois and Eunice, Lydia and Priscilla. These are read only during weekdays in the Easter Season as vehicles to illustrate the wonders worked by Peter and Paul. Is it any wonder, then, that women fail to recognise the ministry of their foremothers?

Since the Second Vatican Council (1962-65), female scholars have had an increasing interest in the Bible and in the contributions that women made towards furthering the reign of God. They have paid special attention to their capacity for self-sacrifice, spirituality, hospitality and ministry. Our foremothers in faith, who joined the discipleship, committed themselves unconditionally to the Good News. They demonstrate continuity from Nazareth to Jerusalem, Cana to Calvary, the Resurrection Garden to the Mount of the Ascension, and from Pentecost Sunday in the Upper Room to Asia Minor and Rome – the heart of the Empire.

As will be shown below, they never ran away, denied or doubted Jesus; nor did they shy away from hardship, persecution or prison. They established house churches in their homes; 'broke bread' with their local faith communities; gave hospitality to their co-workers; and spent their lives carrying out the Works of Mercy with untiring dedication (Mt 25: 35-36). In his commentary on the Letter to the Romans, St John Chrysostom wrote: "[What] an honour we have, in that there are such women among us, but we are put to shame, in that we men are left far behind by them… For the women of those days were more spirited than lions." (taken from: *Biblical Affirmations of Women* by Leonard Swidler, p.295).[1]

All the women portrayed in the following pages are recorded, in either *The Acts of the Apostles* or the *Letters of Paul,* as holding special ministries. Lydia is the only woman named as having been converted directly by Paul. Dorcas, Rhoda, Euodia and Syntyche, Sapphira, Lois and Eunice, Priscilla, Nympha, Chloe, Phoebe and Junia, were 'foreigners' who embraced the Good News on or after Pentecost Sunday in Jerusalem (Acts 2:8-10). They were single women, mothers, daughters, grandmothers, wives, widows, traders and homemakers. None of them had walked with Jesus in either Galilee or Judea.

Their stories demonstrate the wonderful way in which the Holy Spirit worked in God's people following the first Pentecost. Furthermore, they invite us to reflect on our response to the Holy Spirit as, standing together in this first decade of the third millennium we aspire to become a new Pentecost People. What better way to do this than to journey prayerfully with these powerfully dynamic and faith-filled women? Why not let them and their stories challenge us in our time? They have so much to teach us about our dignity as daughters and sons of God; about flawed humanity, our need to listen to the Holy Spirit in our lives; and about prayer, justice, fidelity, mercy and collaboration in the ministries of hospitality, witness and proclamation.

NOTES

1   In my research the version of this quotation I found began with the word '*For*'. As this takes from the sense of the second phrase of the sentence, I have substituted the word 'What'. *For* may be a misprint.

Mary: A Model and an Inspiration for All Ages and Cultures

And he came to her and said,
"Hail, O favoured one, the Lord is with you!"
Lk 1:28

Born into Old Testament Times and bridging the gap between the two great Testaments, Mary of Nazareth is easily the most celebrated woman in Christian history. Over the millennia she has become a global icon. As Mother of the earth's most famous Son she has attracted the attention of the world's greatest scholars, theologians, artists, iconographers, sculptors, musicians, novelists, film producers and the media alike. Each has sought in her or his own way, to enlighten humanity about the relevance of her life not only for the Christian but for all faith communities.

Our library shelves have, until recent years, been filled with androcentric literature which portrayed her as the pious, humble and subservient young girl who despite being specially chosen by God to become the mother of his Son, lived out her life as the hidden and obedient wife of Joseph, a simple carpenter in Galilee. "On balance this ideal has functioned effectively to keep women in their preassigned place subordinate to patriarchal authority."[1]

The male ego has been facilitated by this portrayal

of Mary. It has made her appear as the perfect female whose favourite words were, 'Let it be done unto me according to your word.' The 'word' here, of course, was intended to assign her and all women a place as subordinate. However, it cannot be denied that Mary's motherhood has been of world-changing significance.[2]

As mother of our Saviour, Jesus Christ, and of the Pentecost church, Mary has been honoured in the Church as Advocate, Helper, Benefactress, and Mediatrix.[3] Her intercession has been sought through the ages by both men and women alike. However, since the days of the Second Vatican Council there has been a noticeable diminishment in western society in this devotion which once stood at the heart of every Catholic family, parish and school. Each age, indeed each nation, has sought to depict Mary in a way that speaks to its own culture, to its social, political, and economic situation and to its future hopes. Our age does not seem to know how to image Mary anymore. Having become newly affluent and sophisticated, we seem to have lost something precious in our spirituality and piety.

However, new gynocentric interpretations of scripture are bringing to life the truly feminine, liberating virtues and leadership qualities of Mary. This is tremendously helpful to the women of this new millennium who, possibly without recognising it, have a genuine need for a fully human, strong and dynamic role model. Contemporary female scholars recognise their duty to do for the women of our age what men of past millennia did for men in theirs. They are called to bring to life afresh this vigorous, faith-filled, versatile, steadfast and subversively liberating woman who has the grace to conquer darkness in all its contemporary forms.

Despite the prosperity which being first world nations has provided for us, it has failed to satisfy our search for wholeness, fidelity, justice, compassion, harmony and peace. These qualities are to be found distinctively and abundantly in Mary. Deep in its sub-conscious our current all-embracing, self-sufficient, pluralistic, newly affluent and economically flourish-ing western society is pleading for the love, friendship, motherly virtues of care, hope, protection, com-passion, steadfastness and simplicity which are only to be found in Mary. Could our generation be helped to wholeness if it could be partnered in a pilgrimage with her through the Gospels?

In the first chapter of Luke's Gospel which is often referred to as the Gospel of women, we are introduced to Mary, a young teenager alone in Nazareth. She is betrothed to Joseph of the House of David, and contemplating her forthcoming marriage. Her life is about to be transformed without either preparation or warning. Luke situates her in the presence of angel Gabriel who is delivering a special message to her from God: She has been chosen to bring the promise made to David of a descendent, who would be anointed king and messiah, to fulfilment (2 Sam 7:1-17). Her motherhood, Gabriel tells her, will have everlasting consequence. In short she has been chosen to be God's human agent in the redemption of humanity. Luke devotes the rest of this Gospel to demonstrating how, in time, this came about and how Jesus, Mary's Son lived and worked throughout his life under the direct guidance of his Father, the Divine Agent, in all things. He also makes clear that Mary was always close to her Son's side and that his liberating mission became her mission too.

John supports Luke's presentation of Mary as ever there for Jesus and his disciples throughout his ministry by noting that, *"standing by the cross of Jesus were his mother..."* (Jn 19:25). This is no ordinary mother. This is a woman with a message for women and men of all ages and races. She is the faithful one, the intercessor for those in need and the prophet who had predicted justice for the poor and liberation for the oppressed (Lk 1:51-53). She who had been declared 'favoured one' (Lk 1:28); blessed (Lk 1:42); Woman (Jn 2:4); hearer and doer of the word (Lk 8:21); and finally, woman and mother (Jn 19:26,27), continues to have a central nurturing and sustaining role at the heart of her Son's church today.

This role which was confirmed by Jesus as he hung on the cross had first been conferred on her by God when Gabriel greeted her:

> *And he came to her and said, "Hail, O favoured one, the Lord is with you!"* Lk 1:28

Luke tells us that Mary was perplexed when she heard this greeting. She was a normal Jewish teenager who never thought of herself as different from any of her peers. She was, however, being called to carry out an extraordinary mission for God's people. No wonder this unexpected and uninvited salutation frightened her. However, Gabriel was quick to empathise with her, and to explain that the favour in which she was held by God resulted from the fact that from all eternity, Divine Providence had ordained that she

was to be the human mother of God's Son, Jesus –
the promised Messiah. The time for God to make
this great intervention in human history has now
arrived and Mary was being invited by God to accept
the privilege, challenge, responsibility and blessing.

Her response demonstrated that she was a
uniquely graced human being. Even if a little per-
turbed initially, she readily accepted and in so doing
secured herself a permanent and distinctive place
in God's plan for the restoration of humanity. This
acceptance would bring her, like all women who
make unconditional commitments to marriage, the
single celibate, or consecrated life, and embrace motherhood at physical or spiritual levels, the unexpected
in abundance.

She had no idea what lay ahead of her. She agreed
to a voyage the destination of which was totally
unknown to her. She was about to set sail alone on a
sea that would demand exceptional navigational skills.
She would cruise on beautifully calm waters. She
would also have to battle with storm force gales and
be tossed about by forces greater than any modern
hurricane. She was alone. Her sole security was her
solid confidence in God.

She would be the one who would give birth while
the angelic choirs serenaded her with greetings of
glory and peace. She would see the simple shepherds
bow in reverence before her new-born Son. She
would accept precious and symbolic gifts from kings
on his behalf. She would be instrumental in having
him change water into wine at the wedding in Cana.
She would be elevated to the position of Mother of
his church at the foot of the Cross; be a witness
to the Resurrection in the Upper Room; and be

confirmed and re-commissioned for ministry by the Holy Spirit on Pentecost Sunday. All of this would happen in time. For now it was hidden and would only be revealed as and when she had the strength to engage with, and embrace it.

She would be empowered to reach beyond self, embrace the unexpected, the unpalatable, rejection, pain of loss, exclusion and the crucifixion of her only Son. She would be the one to hold his broken body in her arms and to witness his burial in a borrowed tomb. Had she known what was ahead of her would she have had the strength to accept it?

Almost in an instant she would leave her girlhood behind and become a woman who though sustained by a profound faith, would feel a great need for privacy, affirmation and security. These were needs that she would experience in plenty in the years ahead. In the immediate future she could turn to her aged cousin Elizabeth, who, Gabriel told her, had herself, miraculously conceived a child and was already three months pregnant (Lk 1:36).

Many interpreters describe Mary's visit to Elizabeth as the charitable act of a caring young woman reaching out to a pregnant and needy elderly relative. Such a motive is praiseworthy, but it is cancelled out by the fact that Mary left her cousin again before the actual birth and at the time when she most needed the help of an innovative, caring and loving relative. Theologically, in bringing Mary to Elizabeth's house:

"Luke brings together two mothers-to-be (1:25 and 1:36), so that both might praise God active in their lives and that Elizabeth's child might be presented as the 'precursor' of Mary's child. Luke removes Mary from the scene before the birth of John, so that each birth narrative might have solely the three main characters proper to it: Zachariah, Elizabeth, and John; Joseph, Mary and Jesus."[4]

Through the gift of the Holy Spirit Elizabeth understood John's reaction to Jesus in terms of the liberation and freedom of God's people as in the liberating stories of Jael's people (Judg 5:24) and Judith's (Jdt 13:18). Elizabeth affirmed Mary calling her blessed and *"the mother of my Lord"* (Lk 1:43). This would have been the confirmation that the human Mary needed to support her in her new role and mission. It is essential that we always remember that it was Jesus who was both human and divine and that Mary, despite being his mother, was as human as any of her peers. Unlike them she had been predestined to carry out an extraordinary mission.

Elizabeth's declaration of Mary's blessedness and her confirmation of the presence of Jesus within her, motivated this initially meek girl to express her joy and her praise of God for the graces given to her; and the mercy extended to humanity through her (Lk 1:46-50). Having acknowledged the power and compassion of her God in the first stanza of her beautiful *Magnificat*, Mary demonstrated something of her depth of insight into God's relationship with humanity. She voiced aloud and with deep feeling, the desire of Divine Providence for freedom and justice for the poor. In her new-found subversively liberating and prophetic style, she announced God's power to bring about a reversal of rank between the rich and those whom they deprived of their rights while refusing to acknowledge the power of the

Almighty (1:51-55). Thirty years later Mary would hear her Son echo some of these sentiments in the synagogue in Nazareth when he adopted words from Isaiah in his own mission statement:

> *The Spirit of the Lord is upon me, because he has anointed me to preach good news to the poor. He has sent me to proclaim release to the captives and recovering of sight to the blind, to set at liberty those who are oppressed, to proclaim the acceptable year of the Lord.* Lk 4:18-19

Mary entered the home of Elizabeth as a faith-filled and God-centred young woman who saw herself as lowly. This may have been because of her pregnancy and betrothed as opposed to married status. She left, a self-assured mother-to-be, conscious that she had been "empowered by God to act as an agent in his exaltation of the lowly".[5] Her Magnificat would become her mission statement and she would ensure that her Son made the principles enshrined therein the centre of his life's work.

In time both women gave birth to their sons and nurtured them in their Jewish faith, prayer life and spirituality. Eventually the boys became men and, having discerned what God was calling them to in life, they left home. John began his ministry in Judea preaching a baptism of forgiveness. There Jesus visited him and was baptised by him in the river Jordan before being confirmed by the Holy Spirit in the words: *"Thou art my beloved Son; with thee I am well pleased"* (Lk 3:22b). The descent of the Holy Spirit on Jesus at this moment in time signified the beginning of something new for humanity. It parallels the breath of the Spirit over the waters at the moment of creation in the book of Genesis. As Jesus came up out the waters of the Jordan, God sent the Holy Spirit upon him indicating that a new creation was about to begin. Jesus, the new Adam would restore humanity to its God. John as the last of the Old Testament prophets and the first of the New had carried out the work given to him. Elizabeth's son would gradually withdraw from the centre stage and Mary's would replace him on an equally gradual basis.

Filled with the Holy Spirit, Jesus returned to Galilee where, with his disciples, he joined his mother at a wedding in Cana. There he would give the first sign that the old creation has passed away and that he had been anointed to generate something new (Jn 2:1-2).

When the wine failed, the mother of Jesus said to him, *"They have no wine." And Jesus said to her, "O woman, what have you to do with me? My hour has not yet come." His mother said to the servants, "Do whatever he tells you."* (Jn 2:2-5).

On noticing that the wine had run out and the young couple appeared to be in danger of embarrassment, Mary turned to her Son for help. This was his opportunity to begin his new work and to demonstrate that he was committed to his mother's mission statement.

As though surprised by her intervention, he appeared to challenge her: *"O woman, what have you to do with me? My hour has not yet come."* Having been claimed by the Father at the Jordan (Lk 3:22b), Jesus was making clear that, "no human agency, only the Father's will guides what Jesus does in his ministry."[6] He would facilitate Mary's indirect request but it would be because he was obedient to the Father alone and as a consequence all humanity would be subject to him. In highlighting his '*hour*', and then having Jesus yield to Mary's indirect request, John is portraying Jesus as giving the first hint of a link between the wedding at Cana, his death on Calvary, the empty tomb and Mary's role in the work of salvation, to his mother.

Once again John appears to be drawing a parallel with the Genesis story. In chapter three we read the account of 'The Fall'. The first woman, Eve, was tempted by the devil to disobey God in order to gain sovereignty over all things. She proceeded to engage her husband as a partner. God discovered their sin and cast them out of paradise but not without a promise of redemption. Interestingly, the promise was to be fulfilled through the woman. *"I will put enmity between you and the woman, and between your seed and her seed; he shall bruise your head, and you shall bruise his heel"* (Gen 3:15). In John, the first woman, the old Eve who sought power and control, had now been succeeded by another woman, Mary, the new Eve. She sought to assist. Protection of the dignity of her fellow human beings was her priority. She was a woman for others. She, Mary had given birth to Jesus the new Adam and now she was inviting him to seek not sovereignty for himself but to render service to humanity.

It is worth noting that John has Jesus refer to his mother as "woman", *ishah* in Hebrew, the word Adam used for Eve at the moment of her creation (Gen 2:23). His intention appears to be to introduce his readers to the new Adam and the new Eve. John's new Adam was about to do something new – to restore humanity to its original dignity and relationship with God. The work of redemption was about to begin in Cana. It was the privilege of the woman to invite her Son to embark on the mission which had been God's plan for him from the beginning.[7]

Mary's indirect request to her Son demonstrates that her years of pondering on Gabriel's promise and Simeon's prophecy had led her to faith in her Son. He had appeared to have rejected her indirect urge to rescue the couple who in John symbolise, humanity. However, it was clearly the Father's will that this was the moment for his inauguration into ministry. With admirable discretion, timing and simplicity, Mary had found the right occasion for Jesus' induction. "It was a single incident but it had a universal dimension. It underlined not just Mary's temporary influence at Cana, but her permanent role in the economy of salvation."[8] Simeon had given a universal dimension to Jesus future ministry (Lk 2:32); from now on Mary would be his loyal and faithful disciple as he set off from Cana to pursue that mission.

This first miracle signalled to his disciples that Jesus was no ordinary human rabbi. With them he left Cana and travelled with his mother to the Galilean town of Capernaum (Jn 2:12b). Matthew confirms that Jesus made Capernaum, a town that is mentioned fifteen times in the Synoptics, his base (Mt 4:13). From there at appropriate intervals, he journeyed to and from Jerusalem, which was the goal of his ministry, until his 'hour' arrived, and such visits culminated in the giving of himself in death there, during the Passover festival three years later.

In the light of fact that Mary, moved with him to

Capernaum, it is clear that in good times and in bad, she was present. With the other women disciples, she supported him with her love; comforted him in his trials; tried to protect him when his liberating teaching was rejected and his life was in danger from those who felt that their positions of power were under threat. It was she who provided a comfortable home, a listening ear, a discerning but never over-powering heart and a warm welcome when he returned from his ministry in need of rest, affirmation, consolation and renewal.

And he was told, *"Your mother and your brothers are standing outside, desiring to see you." But he said to them, "My mother and my brothers are those who hear the word of God and do it."* (Lk 8:20-22; Mt 12:50; Mk 3:35).

Mary held a very public role in her Son's mission. All three evangelists record her concern for him as expressed in this passage. As at Cana, while conscious of his mother's human care and grateful for her support, Jesus was particularly attentive to his Father's will. He knew that his mother was an understanding disciple. She had heard the word of God, kept it and acted on it (Lk 1:38). Conscious of this truth, instead of excusing himself from his immediate engagement with the crowd to speak to her, he turned the disciples' point of information into a challenge. He invited them and all those listening to him to follow Mary's example and make a commitment to the Gospel. In short, he explained to them that a human relationship with him was open to everyone; but that for such a relationship to be fruitful and meaningful it must be grounded in a faith commitment like Mary's.[9] She was his paradigm and the model by which others ought to measure their faith and dedication to making the Kingdom of God a reality in the world.

Having assured us that Mary was never far from Jesus the evangelists take for granted that their readers recognise that whenever the women disciples are in ministry with Jesus, she is there at the centre. There is, therefore, no reason to keep on itemising her presence unless, that in her role as 'Mother of Jesus', she is seen to make a unique and distinctive contribution to the life and ministry of the group. Her presence at the foot of the cross was certainly one such occasion.

> *When Jesus saw his mother, and the disciple whom he loved standing near, he said to his mother, "Woman, behold, your son!" Then he said to the disciple, "Behold, your mother!" And from that hour the disciple took her to his own home.*
>
> Jn 19:26-27

The Synoptic Gospels name various women who travelled with Jesus to Calvary. They tell us that while the male disciples fled, these women stood at a distance from the cross (Mt 27:55-56; Mk 15:40; Lk 23:27,55). John, also, names members of the group and presents them standing, *"Near the cross of Jesus"*. However, he singles out *"his mother"* as standing close to the cross with her sister, *"Mary the wife of Clopas, and Mary Mag'dalene"* (Jn 19:25). As she stood there Mary was fulfilling a number of roles. She was: mother of the accused, carer for the condemned, chief mourner, paradigm of fidelity, campaigner against injustice and victim of Jerusalem and Rome's greatest recorded act of treachery. Yes, she was heartbroken as any mother would have been, but she held her grief with dignity. She stood firm both in stature and in commitment. Throughout her life she had learned that suffering is part of the human journey of every person on life's pilgrimage. She knew Divine Providence carries those who bear their burdens with faith. She had given him life, inducted him into ministry, encouraged him in his liberating work and she shared in his mission statement. She had always been strong for him and she would not fail him now.

Unknown to her and to all those who accompanied her, she was about to have her status elevated and her responsibilities increased by her Son. He had appreciated her fidelity and her love. He knew that she would continue to be faithful to his mission when, in his humanity, he was no longer available to walk physically amongst God's people. He knew too, that as her only Son, he had a responsibility to ensure that she had a secure future and a position that would enable her to continue that liberating work of which she had spoken during her visit to Elizabeth. He remembered her urging at Cana that he make it his own. He knew that it was because of his fidelity to this cause that he was now undergoing the most shameful death. As the calm, all embracing and forgiving victim of Rome's most horrendous crime, inhumanity and vulgarity, he spoke to his mother and the beloved disciple, saying: *"Woman, behold, your son!" Then he said to the disciple, "Behold, your mother"* (Jn 19:26-27).

He addressed her as 'Woman' just as he had done at Cana. Bearing in mind the fact that John's Gospel is frequently referred to as the Gospel of signs and symbols and that it is open to many layers of interpretation, it seems reasonable to postulate that he was once more referring to the Genesis story and God's promise of salvation (Gen 3:15). The use of the word 'Woman' here refers again to Mary, the new Eve. She was the woman through whom redemption was to be achieved. Satan was only able to *"strike the heel"* of Jesus, a temporary swipe. Jesus would however, strike the serpent a fatal blow on the head by rising on the third day.[10]

Jesus' ministry focused on creating a new and life-giving faith community in Jerusalem; a community which would, after Pentecost encircle the globe. At the heart of the Jesus community, Mary had always stood strong. Now, as Jesus neared his end, he entrusted that community to her motherly care. "Jesus' mother represents continuity with Jesus' earthly ministry, and the Beloved Disciple represents the believing community of the present and future".[11] Having commissioned his mother and secured the future of the church, he died.

Significantly, when the soldiers desiring to ensure that he was truly dead pierced his side blood and water flowed out – symbols of life and of the Sacraments. Again Mary was a witness to this as she waited for the body to be released for burial. She had given him life and now she watched while he gave that life for the redemption of God's people whom he had entrusted to her care.

This was the woman around whom the disciples would gather after the burial of Jesus. She was also the woman in whose presence he would reveal himself to them after his Resurrection. Furthermore she was the woman around whom they would assemble in prayer after the Ascension, while they awaited the Holy Spirit whose power would usher in a new age of the story of salvation (Mk 16:16-20; Lk 22:20; 1 Cor 11:25). The new Eve was determined to take her commission seriously and to carry on caring for others, freeing them from unnecessary burdens, and ensuring that they carried on the redeeming ministry of Jesus compassionately and faithfully (Jn 2:5).

Mary of Nazareth, far from being the subservient wife and mother portrayed by medieval to twentieth century writers and theologians grew to become a dynamic, discerning, strong and powerful woman. She took her post Calvary and Pentecost responsibilities as mother, nurturer in the faith, campaigner for social justice and liberator seriously. As a paradigm of faith, hope and love for our sophisticated and affluent, yet often empty, despairing, decadent and dysfunctional western world, she stands out as a committed social and spiritual reformer. She is a beacon of hope and an inspiration to all women and men in this third millennium. Her mission statement has eternal significance. Along side her Son's it represents the finest guide for the future of redemptive leadership in the spiritual, social, political, economic and domestic spheres of our planet.

REFLECTION

When Mary accepted God's invitation to become the Mother of Jesus, she agreed to accept the role of God's human agent in challenging the ideas and expectations of God's people. Her Son would usher in a new age, a new value system and a new interpretation of the Covenant. He would make clear that while the Jewish interpretation of the Law was to be affirmed, its key purpose was to liberate rather than to condemn. Yes, God was and would continue to be a God of justice but from now on that justice would be tempered with loving compassion.

As Pope John Paul II said in his Encyclical: *Redemptoris Mater* (1987), "The Annunciation was the culminating point of Mary's faith in her awaiting of Christ, but is also the point of departure from which her whole 'journey toward God' begins, her whole pilgrimage of faith."[12] Believers from all the world's great religions acknowledge Mary's faith and the sacrifices she made for humanity. Artists have tried valiantly to encapsulate this faith down through the ages and have achieved some powerful results.

However, some overly pious beliefs have led to tinselled, synthetic, unreal and unhelpful portrayals of the Mother of God. These, together with a lack of understanding of the Church's teaching, have contributed to modern scepticism, disengagement and to a lack of devotion to Mary.

Mary was the first to notice the plight of the young couple at Cana and the first to take action to save them embarrassment and to ensure that their wedding day would be enjoyed and remembered with gratitude.

• Is enough done in our homes, schools and parishes to demonstrate the power of the compassionate, empathetic and caring Mary in our day?

The young Mary rushed to her cousin Elizabeth with the wonderful, yet frightening news of her pregnancy.

She needed the understanding and support of an older faith-filled woman. Elizabeth, who also walked with God, affirmed Mary and gave her the courage to go forward in faith but also helped her to see herself and all those faithful women who would succeed her in a new relationship with God and the world.

- Surely this woman is in a unique position to reach out to modern teenage girls and young women when they are faced with life changing decisions?

- Is not this the woman who knows how to intercede with her Son for the women and men of our time and culture who are searching in their brokenness for understanding, compassion for-giveness, friendship and wholeness?

- Is not she the one who sees our real needs and longs to introduce us to Jesus who loves, liberates, reconciles and pours out mercy?

Has the time come when we need artists, theologians, pastors and teachers who will provide images of Mary that will speak in a new way to our exteriorly sophisticated, affluent and self-sufficient society, but interiorly crushed, broken and weighted down by unnecessary worries, sin and emptiness?

Let us Pray

Compassionate Mary, you know what it is to feel unsure, alone, and in need of understanding. You trusted God in the midst of fear and darkness. You cared for the young couple at Cana, you found Jesus when he was lost in the Temple. You sought him out when he was exhausted from over work. You supported him on the route to Calvary. You took him to the tomb and you rejoiced with him in the Resurrection Garden. Look with mercy on me in my current frightened, insecure and nervous state. In your love, guide me into the arms of Jesus your Son, so that through him, I may discover my own resurrection garden. Amen.

NOTES

1 Elizabeth Johnson. Truly Our Sister: A Theology of Mary in the Communion of Saints. Continuum, New York. 2003. p. 7.

2 Richard Bauckham. *Gospel Women.* T&T Clark International, London. 2002. p. 59.

3 Gen. Ed. Austin Flannery, O.P. *Vatican Council II: The Conciliar and Post Conciliar Documents* Vol 1, Dominican Publications, Dublin. 1996, §62.

4 Edited by Raymond E. Brown, SS., Joseph A. Fitzmyer, SJ., & Roland E. Murphy, O.Cam. *The New Jerome Biblical Commentary.* Prentice Hall, Englewood Cliffs, New Jersey. 1990, 1968. p. 681.

5 Bauckham, p. 76.

6 Edited by Raymond E. Brown, SS., Joseph A Fitzmyer, SJ., & Roland E. Murphy, O.Cam. *The New Jerome Biblical Commentary.* Prentice Hall, Englewood Cliffs, New Jersey. 1990, 1968. p. 945.

7 Mary Anne Getty-Sullivan. *Women in the New Testament.* The Liturgical Press, Collegeville, Minnesota. 2001. p. 223.

8 + Joseph Cassidy. *These Might Help.* Veritas, Dublin. 2000. p. 189.

9 The Conciliar and Post. Conciliar Documents Vol 1, §58.

10 Father Oscar Lukefahr, CM. *Christ's Mother and Ours.* Liguori, MO. 1998. p. 45.

11 Getty-Sullivan, p. 228.

12 Pope John Paul II, *Redemptoris Mater* (March 25, 1987), § 14.

Mary: Mother, Post Pentecost Pioneer and Partner in Mission

All these [the eleven named disciples] with one accord devoted themselves to prayer, together with the women and Mary the mother of Jesus, and with his brothers... Acts 1:14

In Luke's Gospel Mary forms a bridge between the Old and the New Testaments. She appears as a pioneer of a new age, while at the same time forming an essential link with Judaism. She continues to hold the roles of both bridge and pioneer in the life of her Son, the birth of the Church and our continuing faith journey in discipleship in the third millennium. Luke introduces her as a woman alone who is about to become the Mother of the World's most famous Son.

In his second work "Acts", he again names her but this time as a member of a group – about one hundred and twenty of her Son's followers, men and women who had been members of his discipleship. The new age has dawned and she is continuing her faith journey and pioneering work in the Spirit. "The mention of Mary by name serves a theological purpose for Luke because it establishes continuity between the birth of Jesus and the birth of the early church."[1]

It also allows him to confirm to his readers that

the discipleship remained united and that the mission, which the angel told Mary her Son would fulfil had not changed. It was the work of the Holy Spirit; a work that was ongoing and Mary walking with the Holy Spirit continued to have a stake in it. The fact that none of the other women are named can be taken to mean that Luke, by now inculturated into Roman society, no longer felt as free to affirm women as he had done in his earlier work. "Women were second class citizens in the Roman Empire... Luke shapes his treatment of women in Acts to conform to the Roman model."[2]

> *When the day of Pentecost had come, they were all together in one place. And suddenly a sound came from heaven like the rush of a mighty wind, and it filled the house where they were sitting... And they were all filled with the Holy Spirit and began to speak in other tongues, as the Spirit gave them utterance.*   Acts 2:1,2,4

In this context *"they were all together"* refers to the apostles now twelve again following the election of Matthias (Acts 1:26), together with Mary, her female companions and all those who made up the company and waited in prayer for the promised Holy Spirit (Acts 1:4-5). Although part of this special group, scholars make clear that Mary was in no way an overshadowing presence in relation to the other women. Her relationship with them would have continued in the same way as it did before the days of the Passion, Death, Resurrection and Ascension. She may have gone through another life-changing experience, but she had been there before and she had learned how to lean on her God and on her friends (Lk 1:39). She knew how to extend her arms and her embrace to all who offered love, sympathy and affirmation. She was practised in giving to all who either sought or accepted salvation through Jesus (Jn 2:2-11).

In his Gospel Luke related the story of the annunciation and the overshadowing of Mary by the Holy Spirit. He proceeded to show how that same Holy Spirit overshadowed Jesus at the moment of his baptism in preparation for his ministry and again Mount Tabor in preparation for his forthcoming Passion and Death in Jerusalem (Lk 9:28-36). In his second work, he again cites the Holy Spirit descending on the disciples as they prepare in prayer to carry forward Jesus' mission to the world. In doing this he is using his best theological skills to emphasise that the emerging church is the work of the Holy Spirit and that it has its home in the Trinity.

Furthermore he is making clear that it is gender inclusive and that men and women working together in partnership are charged with bringing the Kingdom to completion (Acts 2:1). It is important to understand that equality in partnership does not mean identity in either gifts or ministry. Whilst all are equal in dignity in God, each is gifted by the Holy Spirit with the graces which she or he needs to fulfil the role in ministry to which God calls them as opposed to the one they might choose for themselves or be allocated by others.

At the beginning of his first work, Luke concentrated on Mary's role; but having introduced Jesus, he was quick to leave his readers to take for granted that she continued in a pioneering partnership in her Son's Galilee story. Likewise in his second book, he makes clear that continuity with Mary is maintained, and then proceeds to focus on the male apostles including Paul who was not, of course, an apostle, in the strict Lukan sense.[3] Luke only makes reference to the contribution of individual women such as Mary, when either male success depended on it or when women were found to be of independent means and already in leadership positions (Acts 9:36-42; 16:6-15,40). Scholars believe that Luke is indicating historical memory here and expects readers to take for granted that Mary continued as a member of the proclaiming community.[4]

The descent of the Holy Spirit generated a new enthusiasm, commitment, vision and urgency to share the Good News. Many of those who were baptised that day (Acts 2:41) needed catechising. Having been elevated to the status of Mother of the entire Christian Community by her Son (Jn 19:26), Mary, who had heard the word of God and kept it, was in an ideal position to support this work as a catechist (Lk8:21). Luke saw catechesis as a key ministry and indeed the purpose of Acts was to make clear that the disciples made witness to the Gospel their priority. Acts confirms the trustworthiness of the Gospel story and the Holy Spirit's continuing power in the world through the discipleship. "According to Luke, the forward march of the gospel as narrated in Acts occurred as a direct result of God's guidance and in accord with the divine will."[5] The catechetical skills of the discipleship in the emerging church were the vehicles chosen by to the Holy Spirit for taking the proclamation of the Good News forward.

As a post Pentecost woman, Mary was a living

witness. She had been amongst the many women who had ministered to Jesus during his life-time, had followed him to Calvary, witnessed his death on the cross, identified the place of burial, discovered the empty tomb on Easter Day, been directed by an angel to *"Go quickly and tell his disciples that he has risen from the dead, and behold, he is going before you to Galilee; there you will see him"* (Mt 28:7); and a recipient of the Holy Spirit in the Upper Room on Pentecost Sunday. "…women were not only extremely instrumental at the most critical moments of Christian history, but the basic creed of Christianity, namely, that after his death Jesus was raised to life, was initiated by women's testimony. They were the first to understand the resurrection faith that is the foundation of the church."[6] They were also the first to be commanded by Jesus to proclaim 'the Good News' and the first to do so (Jn 20:17-18).

It is most likely that, as a mentor to the new community Mary remained in Jerusalem for some years as part of the Upper Room or 'home base' Community, and that she joined Mary the Mother of John Mark in hosting and affirming the missionary disciples when they returned home to be renewed and refreshed before moving out into ministry again (Acts 12:12).

However, the discipleship of equals for which Jesus had worked so hard throughout his ministry and which was so much an integral part of Luke's Gospel seems to be somewhat overlooked in his second book. "Luke is above all a gentleman's gentleman, and Acts is his book".[7] In the light of this it is easy to understand why Acts does not give Mary and the other women the place which would be their right if

38

the book had been written for a non-gender selective readership.

Having been written for the elite in Rome, it stands in sharp contrast to the earlier writings of Paul to his more socially inclusive audience in Rome (Rom 16:1-16), at Philippi (Phil 4:2-3) and at Corinth where women's gifts and spiritual leadership were embraced on an equal footing with their male counterparts. Clearly in Paul's time, which preceded the writing of Acts by about thirty years, the majority of those who put their faith in Jesus came from amongst God's most favoured, the poor (Lk 1:52). Social status was certainly not an issue in Corinth (1 Cor 1:11).[8] Acts, therefore, presents us with both an incomplete account of the spread of Christianity in Europe and the near East, and of leadership in the early days of the church.[9]

Despite this, Mary's role in the salvation story and her place in the discipleship was not forgotten. Paul writing to the Galatians in 57–58 AD emphasises that Jesus' power to save humanity came about because as Son of God and Son of Mary he was both divine and human Gal 4:4-5). In her humanity Mary had given birth to Jesus, one of us, and nurtured him in preparation for his mission. Being one of us he understood our human condition; and as God, he had the power to rescue us thanks to Mary's 'Fiat' (Lk 1:38).

Writing in about the year 95 AD the author of the *Book of Revelation*, which belongs to a collection of literature called Apocalypse, a genre prevalent a couple of hundred years before and after Jesus' birth; and which uses figurative language, symbols and numbers, visions, heavenly messengers, and graphic descriptions of the struggle between good and evil, had a special place for Mary and for her Son according to Catholic interpretations,

> *And a great portent appeared in heaven, a woman clothed with the sun, with the moon under her feet, and on her head a crown of twelve stars; she was with child and she cried out in her pangs of birth, in anguish for delivery. And another portent appeared in heaven; behold, a great red dragon, with seven heads and ten horns, and seven diadems upon his heads. His tail swept down a third of the stars of heaven, and cast them to the earth. And the dragon stood before the woman who was about to bear a child, that he might devour her child when she brought it forth; she brought forth a male child, one who is to rule all the nations with a rod of iron, but her child was caught up to God and to his throne… But the woman was given the two wings of the great eagle that she might fly from the serpent into the wilderness, to the place where she is to be nourished for a time, and times, and half a time. The serpent poured water like a river out of his mouth after the woman, to sweep her away with the flood. But the earth came to the help of the woman, and the earth opened its mouth and swallowed the river which the dragon had poured from his mouth. Then the dragon was angry with the woman, and went off to make war on the rest of her offspring, on those who keep the commandments of God and bear testimony to Jesus.*
>
> Rev 12:1-5 and 14-17a

This passage is open to numerous interpretations, many of them not Christian at all. However, traditionally, Catholics have interpreted the woman as Mary the new Eve, and the mother of the Messiah, Jesus (Gen 3:15). The dragon was seen as a mystic beast and in the East, an image of chaos.[10] Catholics and other Christians see him as Satan and the pangs as the suffering endured by the Church in times of persecution. They are heartened to discover that Christians are forgiven before the heavenly court because of the sacrifice of Jesus. "Vindication in the heavenly court is an ironic reversal of condemnation in the earthly (Roman) courts..."[11] Satan's efforts to destroy the child, Jesus Son of Mary, were doomed because through his resurrection, Jesus conquered death to reign with God.

The woman is also interpreted by some scholars as the Church and *"the rest of her offspring, those who keep the commandments of God and bear testimony to Jesus"*, are the faithful. Christians suffering under the Roman Emperor Domitian (81-96 AD), would have been able to identify themselves and felt comforted and strengthened in their faith and commitment.

Like all mothers Mary had many memories to share with new and enquiring members of the community as they gathered for catechesis, prayer and the breaking of bread. Her recollections and reflections would have challenged, affirmed, inspired and encouraged them. That she had always been a woman of faith and a friend of God, yet forced to carry her own metaphorical 'life-sentence' would have touched them deeply. Despite all the pain and brokenness which she had suffered, they could see that she remained faith-filled and faithful to the commitment she made when a mere slip of a girl, so many years before (Lk 1:38). "...faith involves 'staying with', remaining with Jesus."[12] In listening to her memories and her personal story all new members joining the discipleship could see that Mary, having walked with the Holy Spirit, was indeed a daughter of God, the Mother of the Saviour, a holy woman of faith, a model of discipleship and a compassionate friend to all on life's journey.

In her catechesis she would have reflected on some of the most profound moments in Jesus' life: the washing of the feet at the Last Supper (Jn 13:4-15), and the breaking of bread in particular (Lk 22:19), would evoke feelings of joy, pride, awe, and pain.

Joy, because of the happiness which she had experienced as she watched Jesus leading the prayer and festivities on a night which had such special memories for the people of Israel.

Pride, as she observed the ease with which he exchanged his role as teacher, master and leader for that of servant. He had not forgotten her catechesis on service (Lk 1:46-55 and Jn 2:3-10). She noted that in washing the feet he made no distinction between those of John and Judas. He did not look up to see if the feet he was washing belonged to a saint or a sinner, a woman or a man. All he wanted to do was to serve and to teach the disciples to do likewise. As Walter Brueggemann points out in his book, *Toward A Living Vision*, "The towel and basin are servant tools. They do the work no reputable, competent manager would do – that is, they make contact with dimensions of our humanity that need personal caring attention." She had taught him to serve others. What a delight to reflect on how he had made her lesson part of his most important teachings on that most sacred of nights? Herein lies the greatness of which Gabriel had spoken to her all those years before (Lk 1:32). This was the summation of the Good News. It was to be the Christian way of life.

Awe, at the words he used over the bread and wine: *"This is my body which is given for you. Do this in remembrance of me…This cup which is poured out for you is the new covenant in my blood …"* (Lk 22:19b,20b). She repeated his words: *"This is my body which is given for you. Do this in remembrance of me… This cup which is poured out for you is the new covenant in my blood."* Again the message of service rang in her ears. He was preparing them for the gift which he would make of himself on the cross the following day. His body would be broken; his blood would be poured out in sacrifice and service in order to bring freedom not only to the disciples but to the whole world. He would live forever in the breaking of bread and the pouring of wine (Eucharist), and in imitation of him, his followers would give their lives in the service of broken humanity.

Pain, arising from the devastating events which followed the singing of the final hymn after which he led them out into the Mount of Olives (Mk 14:26-15:47). She had befriended him every step of the way through the streets of Jerusalem and to Calvary. She had tried to be brave for his sake even though at times she felt as though her physical strength would fail and she would join him in his next fall on the ground. A sword had pierced her heart and she had accepted it with the same dignity as she has accepted motherhood from the Holy Spirit (Lk 1:38).

Although nothing is known of the last years of this heroic and pioneering woman's natural life, tradition states that she spent the final period in the company of the beloved disciple to whom the book of Revelation is attributed, and that she was assumed into heaven at the end of her earthly life. Devotion to Mary as intercessor certainly took root in the evolving church from a very early date. This is confirmed by the fact that the prayer, *'Sub Tuum Praesidium',* We fly to thy patronage, O holy Theotokos …, meaning 'Godbearer' or as we in the West say: "We fly to thy patronage, O holy Mother of God …", dates back to 380 AD in the East.

Gradually women are beginning to discover the genuine contribution Mary and her companions made to nurturing and leading the new church. This is enabling them to fashion a life-giving and realistic picture of their spiritual mother and human friend, Mary of Nazareth who having been declared *"favoured one"* by Gabriel (Lk 1:28) and *"blessed"* by Elizabeth (Lk 1:42), had a special reverence for the family and the young (Mt 2:14; Lk 2:4-7; 39-40; 51-52); those in need (Jn 2:1-10); and the harassed and overworked (Mt 12:46; Mk 3:31; Lk 8:20) and finally the Christian community (Acts 1:14). So what had been Mary's contribution to the faith of the people of God?

From Jerusalem, and as Christianity encircled the world, Mary gradually became an international icon, and a model of faith, courage and stamina. She was and continues to be seen as a woman who lived a multi-dimensional life of faith, prayer, listening, service and influence. The challenge which she presented to the waiters at Cana, the service which she rendered to the young couple and the influence which she had with her Son were reflections of what was to come. After the Ascension, grounded in the Trinity and having been commissioned by Jesus she had a unique right to issue that invitation/command: *"Do whatever he tells you"* (Jn 2:5b).

As early as the second century St Justin was drawing comparisons between Eve through whose disobedience humanity was doomed to death through her sin (Gen 2:15-3:24), and Mary whose obedience brought freedom and redemption through Jesus (Lk 1:26-33). St Epiphanius (310-403 AD) declared that while the whole human race was born of Eve, it was truly from Mary that Life was born into the world. So it is as God-bearer, that Mary has been honoured from the earliest day of the church. St Ephem of Edessa (373 AD) prayed to her: "Blessed Virgin, immaculate and pure you are the sinless mother of your Son, mighty Lord of the universe… the hope of the hopeless and sinful; we sing your praise."

At no time in her life did Mary single herself out as special or uniquely holy. In speaking of her status in her Magnificat, she attributed her blessedness to God, *"for he has regarded the low estate of his hand-maiden. For behold, henceforth all generations will call me blessed "* (Lk 1:48). Perhaps that is a reason why in the immediate post apostolic period it was forgotten that a mother and her Son generally come as a 'two-pack'. In Mary's case this was certainly true. They shared a common mission of service as is made clear in Mary's commitment to the poor and in Jesus' own mission statement (Lk 1:48-55 and 4:18). However, It was only after the Council of Ephesus in 431 AD, and the resulting proclamation of the humanity and divinity of Jesus that the Church gave her the title of God-bearer, a title first given to her by Elizabeth (Lk 1:43).

From the time of St Augustine of Hippo to Anselm of Normandy the theory that Mary was born free from original sin was widely promulgated so much so that by the twelfth century a Feast in honour of Mary's Conception was celebrated annually in many European countries including Britain. However, some of the Church's finest scholars had great difficulty with the idea until the great Franciscan theologian Duns Scotus of Scotland (1266-1308), resolved the issue by explaining that the Immaculate Conception was a unique gift of God's application of the grace of Jesus in advance. However, not until 1854 did Pope Pius IX feel able to declare it a doctrine of Catholic faith in the following words:

> "We declare, pronounce, and define that the doctrine which holds that the most Blessed Virgin Mary, in the first instance of her conception, by a singular grace and privilege granted by Almighty God, in view of the merits of Jesus Christ, the Saviour of the human race, was preserved free from all stain of original sin, is a doctrine revealed by God and therefore to be believed firmly and constantly by all the faithful."[13]

In these words the Holy Father made clear as Mary herself did (Lk 1:48) that her blessedness was a special gift of grace from God.

The New Testament does not give any details of Mary's old age or death, and there are no first century records of her burial. From very early time it was believed that because of Mary's Motherhood of Jesus and her fidelity to the Trinity, she was graced by God with the unique privilege of being assumed into heaven. A feast celebrating Mary's Assumption was celebrated in Syria in the fifth century, in Jerusalem in the sixth and in Rome in the twelfth century. From that point onwards there has been a life-giving belief in the Assumption of Mary throughout the universal Church. In 1950 Pope Pius XII gave this indomitable pioneer one of her finest accolades when he declared in the dogma of the Assumption:

"…after we have poured forth prayers of supplication again and again to God, and have invoked the light of the Spirit of Truth, for the glory of Almighty God who has lavished his special affection upon the Virgin Mary, for the honour of her Son, the immortal King of the Ages and the Victor over sin and death, for the increase of the glory of that same august Mother, and for the joy and exultation of the entire Church; by the authority of our Lord Jesus Christ, of the Blessed Apostles Peter and Paul, and by our own authority, we pronounce, declare, and define it to be a divinely revealed dogma: that the Immaculate Mother of God, the ever Virgin Mary, having completed the course of her earthly life, was assumed body and soul into heavenly glory."[14]

It is important to note that the dogma does not attribute this unique privilege to the human Mary so much as it does to give honour to her Son and glory to God the Creator. Once again Mary is thrust in the role of pioneer. Her Assumption is the logical outcome of her immaculate conception. John's vision in Revelation of the woman clothed with the sun, with the moon at her feet and with twelve stars on her head forms a Scriptural foundation for belief in the dogma of the Assumption.[15] The Assumption of this great pioneer, carer, and friend is a huge source of hope to the pilgrim people of God.[16] What happened to Mary will happen to all who having been redeemed by her Son live and proclaim the Good News. The ultimate home of all God's people became a reality in their pioneer, Mary of Nazareth, who having held the discipleship in prayer in preparation for the coming of the Holy Spirit continues to hold all the redeemed before her Son as they prepare to meet him in glory.

REFLECTION

Holy Mother Church has always acknowledged that Mary was a unique human being because of the special privilege conferred on her by God at the moment of the Annunciation. She presents her to us as: Advocate, Helper, Benefactress, and Mediatrix, while at the same time making clear that this in no way diminishes the role of Jesus as our Mediator.[17] Her message to us is that: she, who said "Yes", to the Holy Spirit for our sakes, continues to stand with her Son today as our pioneer, carer, friend and an intercessor. She who was always non-gender selective and always welcoming of the voice of women.

In her book, *Are Men Necessary?* (2005), the well known *New York Times* columnist, Maureen Dowd, reflects on all the voice-of-God characters from media organisations to Church patriarchies and concludes that while the networks may be receptive of women's voices, we can be sure that in the Church the voice of God is most definitely not female. From this it is clear that the post-Lukan Church continues to reverence its ancient inculturation.

We in the west, and as inhabitants of the 'first world', are the children of the most affluent, sophisticated and technologically advanced period in human history. We are also amongst the most ambitious and egotistical of peoples. Whether we are ready to admit it or not we seem to have arrived in this world programmed with a focus on self, social status and money.

In contrast, we have also been blest with the capacity to reach out, to help, to pray for and to journey with others. But is it becoming increasingly true that we often only do that when such Christian activity in no way infringes on our number one priority: me and my own happiness, and leisure? Is it possible that we are in danger of deluding ourselves by thinking that because we put our hands in our pockets when we see a poor person seeking money outside our favourite supermarket, boutique or restaurant, or because we attend Mass on Sundays, or pay quick visits to funeral parlours or cemeteries when neighbours die, we are active Christians? Might we be enlightened if we asked ourselves whether we are following the example of the woman who made provision for the young couple at Cana (Jn 2:3-10) or the rich man in Luke 16:19-26? Overcoming self-obsession is a daily challenge for the Christian.

- Perhaps we could ask ourselves if, in our sophistication and affluence we belong to the generation termed by Archbishop Emeritus, Joseph Cassidy the "inside-out and up-side down Christians", those who have small hearts and big mouths – people who know nothing about their neighbours' wants but everything about their weaknesses?

Could it be that we would be enriched by reflecting that:

- Like her Son, Mary appears to have known nothing about her neighbours' sins but everything about their need for service and support (Lk 1:38).

Her value system meant that she concentrated not so much on:

- capitalism or consumerism as on communication and caring (Mt 12:46; Jn 13:4-14; Lk 22:19, 20)

- career ladders and interest rates as on compassion, sharing and continuing Jesus mission (Acts 1:14, 2:1-4)

- social mobility and keeping up appearances as on the joys, sorrows, pains and surprises of mothering (Lk 2:7; Mt 2:21; Lk 2:42-52; Mk 3:31-35; Jn 19:25 and Acts 1:14)

- political correctness and sophistication as on simplicity of life-style, sacrifice, service, solitude and prayer.

We must be very careful, while giving her all the praise and honour due to her as Mother of Jesus and the Church, not to put this pioneer, carer, intercessor and friend on such a high pedestal that our children feel she is unreal, irrelevant to today's challenges and coming to them from another age. The Fathers of the Second Vatican Council warned theologians, preachers and the faithful in general, to avoid all exaggerated and false claims about Mary, while at the same time ensuring that they do nothing to detract from her special dignity as Mother of God.[18] Is it possible that that very warning has been mis-interpreted and has contributed to the erosion of much of the mystique which grew up around Mary over the millennia?

We need to reflect afresh on this unique and self-giving woman. Historical memory makes its own special contribution to Mary as Mother of the Church. She was a real woman whose priorities were those of her God, her family and her neighbours. These are timeless values. She has shown us that all others are seasonal, transient and ultimately fruitless.

- Are we a genuinely Post Pentecost faith com-munity? Do we have the fire and dynamism for the Gospel that our foremothers, in faith, had in their time?

Mary was, like the average teenager, young woman and mother, a simple and straightforward human being who was called by God to make her special contribution to the redemption of God's people. Every girl, woman and mother who has walked this world since Mary's time and who continues to journey today, has been and continues to be called to make her own unique contribution to the on-going redemption of God's people. How sad it would be if any of us were to journey in ignorance, to forget or to abandon God's invitation to partnership and proclamation when Jesus has gifted us with his Mother as pioneer, carer, companion, intercessor and friend?

Closing Prayer

Provident God, I thank you for giving Mary to me personally and to all your people as a model of service and of love. I ask for the grace to see her for what she truly is: a woman who cares, loves, and has shown me how to centre in you; how to journey with the Holy Spirit; how to be open to your intervention in my life in whatever form you choose to visit me. Give me the grace to realise that there will be no surprise, joy, pain or sorrow that my Mother Mary, has not experienced before me; and that as she cared for your disciples in the Upper Room, she will care for me too if I allow her into my life. I make this prayer in union with Jesus and the Holy Spirit. Amen.

NOTES

1 Gail R. O'Day. "Acts" in *Women's Bible Commentary*, Eds. Carol A. Newsom and Sharon H Ringe. Westminster John Knox Press, 1998. p. 396.
2 Ibid p. 395.
3 Ibid p. 396.
4 Elizabeth Johnson. *Truly Our Sister: A Theology of Mary in the Communion of Saints*. Continuum, New York. 2003. p. 298.

5 Clarice J. Martin, The Acts of the Apostles in *Searching the Scriptures* Vol 2. Ed. Elizabeth Schüssler Fiorenza. Crossroads Publ., New York. 1994. p. 767.

6 Elizabeth Johnson. *Truly Our Sister: A Theology of Mary in the Communion of Saints*. Continuum, New York. 2003. p. 300.

7 Gail O'Day. "Acts" in *Women's Bible Commentary*, Eds. Carol A Newsom and Sharon H. Ringe. Westminster John Knox Press, 1998. p. 401.

8 Jones, Alexander. General Editor. The Jerusalem Bible (New Testament section). Darton, Longman & Todd, London. 1996. p. 256.

9 Ed. May, Herbert G. *Oxford Bible Atlas*. Oxford University Press, Oxford, 1983. p. 88.

10 Jerome Biblical Commentary. Prentice Hall, Englewood, New Jersey. 1990, 1968. p. 1008.

11 Ibid.

12 Mary Anne Getty-Sullivan. *Women in the New Testament*. The Liturgical Press, Collegeville, Minnesota. 2001. p. 230.

13 Pope Pius IX. *Ineffabilis Deus,* Defining the Dogma of the Immaculate Conception, December 8, 1854. Apostolic Constitution, The Definition.

14 Pius XII. *Munificentissimus Deus,* Defining the Dogma of the Assumption, 1 November 1950. Apos. Const. § 44.

15 Ibid § 27.

16 *Lumen Gentium* § 68.

17 Ibid § 62.

18 Ibid § 67.

Dorcas: Distinguished Disciple, Daughter and Diplomat

Now there was at Joppa a disciple named Tabitha, which means Dorcas. She was full of good works and acts of charity. Acts 9:36

Dorcas is the first woman in the New Testament to be given her Greek name. In Hebrew she was called Tabitha and she lived in Joppa which today is called Jaffa. It was a one-time famous port on the Mediterranean coast of Judea; and a popular destination for Gentile emigrants, migrants and visitors from Greece, Turkey and the surrounding countries. Dorcas, like many of her country folk, who helped the new arrivals to integrate with the local community, was, in keeping with local practice, known by both Hebrew and Greek names. The fact that Luke, who only named prominent women in the Christian community, gave Dorcas both her Greek and Hebrew names indicates that she was a woman of considerable standing in Joppa.

In her we meet the exemplary Christian, a daughter of the Holy Spirit, a post Pentecost member of the extended discipleship, whose life of service was motivated by her faith. Like Abraham she believed and put her belief into action by her good works (Jas 2:23). She was probably one of Philip's first converts and a member of his original church

community at Joppa following the movement of the apostles out from Jerusalem after Pentecost. More particularly, she was a philanthropist and probably the leader of a small Christian community of widows who supported each other spiritually and lived out the Corporal Works of Mercy making Jesus' words, *"Truly, I say to you, as you did it not to one of the least of these, you did it not to me"* (Mt 25:45), their daily motto.

Conscious that the church was the on-going vehicle for the proclamation of the Gospel, Luke writing to impress the wonders of the Gospel on Theophilus, used the story of Dorcas to demonstrate the power of the Holy Spirit continuing to work in the church. In telling the story, therefore, he was not so much emphasising the giftedness or generosity of women in ministry as portraying the continuing miraculous power of Jesus at work in the male disciples. As a faithful daughter and diplomat, Dorcas was a woman "who with her needle embroidered her name ineffaceably into the beneficence of the world".[1]

One of the characteristics of Luke's writing is his need to portray Christianity in continuity with Judaism, a new interpretation and living of the covenant by God's people and as a gift extended to all peoples regardless of gender or race. For him, Dorcas mirrored the God-centred widows who preceded her in faith: the widow of Zarephath whose son was resuscitated by Elijah (1 Kings 17:9-24; Lk 4:26); Anna who spent much of her time in prayer and fasting in the Temple while she awaited the birth of Jesus (Lk 2:36-37); Mary the Mother of Jesus who gave her unconditional yes to God (Lk 1:38); Salome and Mary the mother of James and Joses who both stood at the foot of the cross (Mk 15:40); the widows amongst the women of Jerusalem (Lk 23:27); and those who travelled from Galilee to be with Jesus in the final hours before his death (Mt 27:55). Dorcas had been empowered by the Holy Spirit with the gift of faith and like her ancestors, she witnessed to it by her life of fidelity, prayer and good works.

Though childless herself, by her very life of service she was a womb in which the emerging church was nourished. As the first of Luke's four stories affirming women's service in Acts, this one provides a concrete glimpse of the generosity and genuine goodness of women in the early church.[2] With Jesus, Dorcas could truly say, *"This is my body given for you"* (Lk 22:19). The hands that dispensed alms and made garments were inwardly inspired by Him whose hands were nailed to the tree.[3]

She was neither a prophetess nor a teacher in the formal sense. Yet through her diplomatic skills, her practical service and witness she fulfilled both roles more profoundly than many of the male disciples and scholarly rabbis of her day. As a widow, she had a unique understanding of the plight of the bereaved. She stood shoulder to shoulder with young widows whose fishermen husbands often became the unsuspecting victims of Joppa's often volatile seas and frequently unpredictable and ferocious north winds which dashed boats against the huge rocks. In normal circumstances these boulders helped to create a sheltered harbour. But in stormy weather they proved deadly for fishing crews, and left their dependents destitute and reliant on the charity of the local community (Deut 14:28-29).

She came from a family who made their money when Joppa was a thriving international port in the region which had been occupied by the tribe of Dan. The port had a long history of supporting the ancient faith of the Jewish people having been the harbour through which the cedars of Lebanon had been brought for the building of the first Temple in Jerusalem 961–926 BCE, during the reign of King Solomon. *"...and we will cut whatever timber you need from Lebanon, and bring it to you in rafts by sea to Joppa, so that you may take it up to Jerusalem"* (2 Chr 2:16).

It was also within the region in which the eighth century prophet Jonah received his call from God to go to Nineveh and call its sinful and despised Gentile people to repentance. Instead of obeying the challenge, the prophet went to the port of Joppa, and boarded a ship for Tarshish in an effort to escape God's call. But one of the storms for which the port became well known blew up and disaster threatened. Jonah recognised his weakness and repented for having tried to avoid fulfilling the Divine instruction. God gave his prophet a second chance and under the guidance of the Holy Spirit, Jonah brought the people of Nineveh back to God (Jon 1:1–3:11).

Joppa made history once again in the sixth century after the Temple in Jerusalem was destroyed in 586 BCE by the Babylonians. Its rebuilding was begun by King Cyrus 559–530 BCE, who having defeated the Babylonians committed himself to allowing the God's People who began returning to Jerusalem to have a place of worship once more. *So they gave money to the masons and the carpenters, and food, drink, and oil to the Sido'nians and the Tyrians to bring cedar trees from Lebanon to the sea, to Joppa, according to the grant which they had from Cyrus king of Persia"* (Ezra 3:7).

The port of Joppa was the only natural harbour on the Mediterranean between Egypt and Acco (Ptolemais). It was the main point of access from the Mediterranean to Jerusalem and the surrounding regions throughout the pre-Christian centuries, and until Herod the Great founded the new city and built the port of Caesarea Maritima between the years 22 and 6 BCE. This had a devastating effect on Joppa which was gradually deprived of international trade and in many respects reduced to the status of a fishing port.

The ancient families such as that of Dorcas who had managed their resources carefully and invested their money wisely continued to prosper. Sadly their neighbours and the ever growing population of Gentile immigrants and migrants were not so fortunate. They were forced to try and make a living in their host country from tourism, home crafts and fishing. Women in Joppa were seen as second class citizens. As a woman of faith who knew the connection between her home port, the Scriptures, and God's plan to embrace the Gentile peoples, Dorcas reached out to meet the physical, emotional and spiritual needs of all the women in Joppa regardless of faith or race. She not only wove wool and cotton together, but more importantly, she wove a community of mixed faiths and ethnicity into a united family.

Her success is demonstrated by the fact that when she died suddenly, her companions, both female and male, were inconsolable. Luke records the story as follows:

In those days she fell sick and died; and when they had washed her, they laid her in an upper room. Since Lydda was near Joppa, the disciples, hearing that Peter was there, sent two men to him entreating him, "Please come to us without delay." So Peter rose and went with them. And when he had come, they took him to the upper room. All the widows stood beside him weeping, and showing tunics and other garments which Dorcas made while she was with them. But Peter put them all outside and knelt down and prayed; then turning to the body he said, "Tabitha, rise." And she opened her eyes, and when she saw Peter she sat up. And he gave her his hand and lifted her up. Then calling the saints and widows he presented her alive. And it became known throughout all Joppa, and many believed in the Lord.   Acts 9:37-42

So in response to Peter's prayer and command, God empowered Dorcas to rise and sit up. The word 'rise' as used here does not mean resurrected in the sense in which Jesus was raised to life on the third day (Lk 24:46). His rising to life was to a life that would not terminate in physical death again. Dorcas' rising up on her couch meant that in God's time, she would die a physical death like all of humanity. Peter's raising of Dorcas was, as in the case of Jarius' daughter, the widow's son at Nain and Lazarus', resuscitation. All three were restored to their loved ones and as in the case of Dorcas there was great rejoicing at the wonders God had done amongst the people, and many new members were added to the community of believers. However, as mortal beings and as daughters and sons of Adam and Eve, the only path open to the newly raised in terms of partnership at the Paschal Banquet, prepared for them by Jesus, would be through their human mortality.

In describing the process through which the followers of Dorcas and Peter went, Luke is once again demonstrating continuity between faith, prayer and miracles in the two testaments. Aware that following a period of prayer Elijah raised the son of the widow of Zarephath in an 'upper room' (1 Kings 17:24); that Elisha's prayer for the son of a Shunammite woman was heard and he was raised in an 'upper room' (2 Kings 4:18-36); and that excluding all the mourners except her parents and Peter, James and John from the room Jesus raised Jarius' daughter (Lk 8:42-49), Luke makes clear that Peter excluded everyone from the 'upper room' before kneeling and pleading with God for the restoration of Dorcas. In the story of the restoration of Jarius' daughter, we read: *"Taking her by the hand* [Jesus] *said to her, "Tal'itha cu'mi"; which means, "Little girl, I say to you, arise"* (Mk 5:41). Likewise, Peter commanded Dorcas: *"Tabitha, rise"* (Acts 9:40), and giving her his hand he lifted her up. The similarities are striking and would not have been lost on the mourners.

By relating this miracle performed by Peter in such detail, Luke was making clear that the Spirit-empowered church retained the healing power of Jesus, and that God would bestow it generously on all those who remained faithful and faith filled from generation to generation. More particularly Luke was keen to ensure that the miracles worked by Peter were made known to the people as wonders that evoked praise for God, stimulated faith and increased the discipleship. A new value system of unconditional service, generosity, prayer and sharing had been adopted following the example of Jesus and it was being affirmed and commissioned afresh in Joppa through the persons of Dorcas and Peter.

For Luke the mission to the Gentiles was about to be inaugurated formally. As the anchor of the twelve, Peter had to be the one to take Christianity out beyond Jerusalem, into the lands of the Gentiles and out to the ends of the earth, meaning Rome. In the light of this, scholars believe that Luke was using the Dorcas' miracle as a prelude to the new expansion. The wonder touched the multi-cultural community deeply and news of it spread throughout the entire region. Luke had portrayed Peter as walking in the footsteps of Jesus, thus ensuring continuity between the Master and the apostle. His intention was to integrate Gentile converts into the christocentric plan of history.[4]

He proceeded to tell his readers that Peter was soon invited to the house of a leading and faith-filled centurion named Cornelius in the thriving new and mainly Gentile port of Caesarea. Cornelius being a Gentile had heard about Jesus and had been a man of prayer and almsgiving but had no foundation in the Christian faith. However following the raising of Dorcas, he had been inspired in a vision to send to Joppa for Peter in order to receive instruction. So impressed was he, his household and locality by Peter's account of Jesus' life and work that the entire community received the Holy Spirit and were baptised by Peter.

The reinstatement of Dorcas in an 'upper room' amongst the poor of Joppa, therefore, had far-reaching effects for the infant church. It took a gigantic step forward in the Gentile world. In addition to this the needs of widows, orphans and the vulnerable, as well as the place of women in society were given a new and elevated status. The concept of 'the upper room' had taken on a new and sacred significance at the Last Supper (Lk 22:12). From now on it would become a centre for house churches as the new faith community moved out from Jerusalem and the synagogues and into the hearts of the homes of the people.

Dorcas is the only woman in the New Testament who warranted the designation 'disciple' or *mathetria* in Greek. Luke's mention of her ministry to the 'saints' suggests that she was not gender selective in her good works. She supported women and men equally. Some scholars wonder if by referring specifically to widows only, Luke was trying to minimise the ministry of women in the Church. They point out that he refers to the good works of men as '*diakonia*', ministry as delivered by the seven deacons (Acts 6:3), while referring to Dorcas' service as *"good works and acts of charity"* (Acts 9:36).

More research is needed in this area, but it seems that to interpret Luke in this way is to fail to understand the social and cultural ideologies that confronted him. He was simply using the language of the time and working within the social and political environment in which he found himself trying to witness to the Gospel. That the Gentile church and its teachers did not foster gender selection in order to exclude women from the ministry of deaconess as understood in the first-century church, is made clear by Paul writing in 57-58 AD: *"I commend* to you our sister Phoebe, a deaconess of the church at Cen'chre-ae, that you may receive her in the Lord as befits the saints ..." (Rom 16:1-2). Elizabeth Schüssler Fiorenza confirms this view: "Acts probably reflects historical experience in stressing that women were involved in the Christian missionary movement at every stage of its expansion. Tabitha of Jaffa [Dorcas of Joppa] represents the first stage of expansion."[5]

The challenges presented by the Gospel to the new faith community during Dorcas' days in Joppa, were the same as those confronting the Institutional and local faith community in this the third millennium: to journey in faith with each developing culture; and to embrace all that is good, supportive of faith and community in keeping with the values of the Carpenter from Nazareth within that culture. Where there are deficiencies relating to gender, race, justice, giftedness, theology or doctrine; it is the duty of leadership in consultation with the faithful to resolve them. In short, each culture was and continues to be called upon to live the Corporal Works of Mercy authentically, knowing as Dorcas did that: *"whatever you do to one of the least of these my sisters and brothers, you do to me"* (Mt 25:40).

REFLECTION

The early church was fired by the Holy Spirit. Dorcas is a model of all that was best in that church. She was centred in the Holy Spirit who makes a home in the heart before ever entering the head. This is verified by: the response of the first disciples to the call of Jesus (Mk 1:16-20); the repentance by Zacchaeus (Lk 19:2-10) and the conversion of Pilate's wife (Mt 27:18-19). The ability to reach out to others in service on a consistent and continuous basis is a call and a gift from the Spirit. It demands utter dedication and unconditional commitment. Anyone can be charitable on a special occasion, over a short period of time or when it suits them. Self-promoting women and men alike, can be quick to find excuses to withdraw when service becomes either inconvenient of when a more attractive option presents itself.

- In what ways did Dorcas show that she had received the gifts of the Holy Spirit?

- If you took 'time out' occasionally to reflect on the gifts and fruits of the Holy Spirit in your life might you be more Gospel-centred women and men in the way you live, act and work?

Care for widows and orphans had its roots in the Old Testament (Ex 22:22; Deut 26:12). They were to be supported by the local community. Because of the emphases which have been rightly placed on the generosity and service of Dorcas to widows and orphans, her holistic ministry to the community or as Luke writes, 'the saints' (9:41), has often been minimised. It has been interpreted as women-to-woman service. When Luke says that she was full of good works, he is telling his readers that she was graced with the gifts and the fruits of the Holy Spirit in abundance. In short, she was absolutely holistic in her ministry to humanity.

When Dorcas died the women and the saints washed her body and anointed it with tender loving

care. Then they laid it out on a bed in the 'upper room' in keeping with the cultural traditions of the time. Having completed the domestic rituals, they assembled in prayer and mourning in keeping with the Jewish customs and in reverence for the dead person. Memories were shared and stories were told. All of this helped the bereaved family members to process their grief and to refocus on life with an attitude of acceptance of the death, and with thanksgiving for a life that had been a gift to the community.

The laying out of a Christian body has, traditionally, been a very sacred ministry in the Church. In Catholic circles the body was laid out in the home, unless the person died in hospital. This was done either by intimate family members or some carefully selected members of the parish. A distinctive habit in brown, blue or black bearing religious symbols that had a special meaning for the deceased person was purchased and placed on the prepared body. The person's hands were joined in a praying position enfolding either rosary beads or a crucifix.

The bed was adorned with white sheets and covers; a table bearing a crucifix, holy water and two lighted candles were placed near the bed. Chairs were arranged alongside the bed for those who would like to sit for a while with the body. The curtains in the room were kept closed, the door was opened and the family and community were invited to visit for short periods in prayer. Meanwhile hospitality was offered to other members of the faith community assembled in support of the bereaved. Food was shared, tales were told, and family members were helped to mourn and to give thanks to God for a life well lived. All of this was done in faith and in imitation of the Jewish Taharah (burial rites), which were profoundly reverent and deeply spiritual rituals. Furthermore, it was carried out in imitation of the reverence shown by the community to Dorcas (Acts 9:37-42), and to the body of Jesus following his crucifixion (Lk 23:53-56; 24:1-4; Jn 19:38-42).

Sadly in our post modern age this practice has nearly disappeared. Nowadays, as soon as life had been certified to have left the body, it is removed to a mortuary. Preparation of the body for burial is handed over to the undertakers. Frequently, even in Religious Communities, the handing over of religious symbols such as rosary and or a crucifix is overlooked. The family may or may not assemble at the mortuary a couple of hours before either the remains are taken to a church or to a crematorium. There seems to be a need to get through the process as quickly and as efficiently as possible.

There is little time for mourning or story telling and the people to suffer in the long term are the bereaved members of families who, because of the new cultural constraints, have not made provision for adequate space, spiritual support and time to grieve. The whole idea of a burial shroud has been dispensed with as have, in many cases, religious symbols. These are often replaced by secular objects or tokens from the worlds of sport, luxury, or enter-tainment and occasionally include perfumes, pictures, letters, cigarettes and miniatures of alcohol. Although family members engage ceremoniously with this new culture; and appear to cope well with its rituals in approaching death, one frequently learns later of great emotional turmoil and problems with readjusting to life. These are frequently the effects of lack of faith, understanding of the spiritual dimension of life and death, and delayed and unprocessed grief.

- Are there lessons that we could learn from our predecessors in faith about ritualising death, about mourning and about grief?

- Docs the fact that recently some members of a Catholic Religious Community of women found it necessary to make a request to their Leadership to have their care home managements notified that all members of the Congregation who die in care must be given a Catholic funeral surprise us?

- Might there be a need in our parishes for our clergy to speak to their communities from time to time about Christian funeral rituals and Christian care for those who have no immediate blood relations?

In her work Dorcas nurtured 'the saints' in general and widows in particular in body, mind and spirit. There are eighty-seven references to 'the saints' between the two testaments. From this it is clear that those who lived justly regardless of gender were referred to as saints throughout both Hebrew and Christian times. It is a misrepresentation of Dorcas' work to limit her ministry solely to the female gender. Two male disciples were sent to Lydda for Peter when Dorcas died. This is clear evidence that she reached out to all who were in need and that they valued her work.

She was a Spirit-centred person. All those who shared ministry with her were moved by her faith actions, and compassion. They were also motivated by the Holy Spirit whom they invited to work in their lives and who brought them to faith in Jesus. Her catechetical teaching to them was practical and her prayer was constant. It is most likely that Dorcas hosted a small community of widows in her own house as a prototype of religious community as we know it. There she would have taught the women dressmaking and other skills in needlecraft in order to produce clothes for those in need. This thinking is supported by the fact that when Peter arrived: *"All the widows stood beside him weeping, and showing tunics and other garments which Dorcas made while she was with them… Then calling the saints and widows he presented her alive"* (Acts 9:39, 41). Had they not shared a common home and lifestyle, it is unlikely that they would have felt at home in her 'upper room'. It is also doubtful that Luke would need to mention them as a separate group from *'the saints'* when relating how Peter presented her to her next of kin, and the community of believers, if they were not more than an ad hoc group (Acts 9:41).

Those women and men, who model their lives on Dorcas for example in 'Dorcas Aid International', make availability and constancy in ministry a priority. They are, like their patron, Spirit-centred individuals who nourish both the souls and the bodies of those to whom they minister. They are givers of hope and their actions prefigure, and enable others to prepare in faith for the Paschal Banquet. They calm the violent seas and smooth the rough boulders of Joppa in the lives of the metaphorically shipwrecked.

Genuinely committed Christian workers today, strive to provide a safe haven for slum dwellers, migrants, asylum seekers and refugees. They pause to *'write on the ground'* while misguided teenagers gain time to reflect on and learn from their mistakes (Jn 8:6-8). They invite victims of abuse to 'rise' and they enable them to stay upright by lending a supporting and affirming hand until they recover that inner healing which only time and prayer can restore. They call the healed, the broken, and the wounded, together with those who are in the process of healing, to mission and ministry. They allow them to grow in the Spirit and in community at a pace that facilitates faith, engenders hope, gives life to love and makes living in a kinship of faith a daily beatitude.

- What is your attitude to migrants, refugees and asylum seekers? Do you see them as trying to live off the charity of others or the State?

- How good are you at affirming the many images of Dorcas in your own homes, parishes and work places today?

Dorcas' heart had been won by the Christian message. She was grounded in the Spiritual Works of Mercy, and her motto was centred in the Corporal Works of Mercy. As a contemplative in action, she was millennia ahead of her time. She was a woman who held a leading position in the faith community. She stands out as a paradigm for women in the twenty-first century. Her story, when interpreted in our modern cultural setting must challenge our current model of leadership and pastoring.

- Might it be possible that Dorcas' story has a message for our current male dominated and hierarchical Church at a time when there is a severe shortage of sacramental ministers and when life long and faith-filled Catholics and members of religious communities both in Europe and on the mission fields are dying without the last sacraments?

- Is there a gap between our mystical embodiment of the Spiritual Works of Mercy and our motivation to give life to them in a practical way through their sisters, the Corporal Works of Mercy?

- Are we aware that it is while 'the saints' are amongst us that we should validate them? Sometimes we wait until they are dead and then write elaborate and emotional yet soulless eulogies when they are already sharers in the Beatific Vision. Do we fail to recognise that they are no longer in tune with our empty words, and that we are simply using them to provide us with a stage on which to massage our own egos?

The concept of 'upper room' had a very special significance for the early church from the night when Jesus instituted the Eucharist in the Upper Room in Jerusalem. As time went by the Christian community were forced to leave the synagogues and to find new places for their worship and prayer. Wisely they began to meet in each others homes and often referred to their meeting place and sacred space as 'the upper room'. The concept of domestic Church as outlined in *Lumen Gentium* § 11, had not yet been established,

but the emerging community knew and understood its role and value in their lives. They met in their own and in each others houses for prayer and the breaking of bread. We can be sure that this practice was very much part of the ritual followed by Dorcas with her community.

- Where is your 'upper room' and how is it decorated and cared for?

- When you 'break bread' together as a community or as a private family are you conscious of the sacredness of the action and of its power to renew and refresh the faith not only of your family but of all those who have the privilege of being guests at your table?

- Are you aware of the value of family prayer and creating little rituals around meals during the various liturgical seasons in an effort to stimulate family faith and as a reminder of the sacredness of such occasions?

Every Christian family is called to contribute to each of the seven elements of Church life: study of the Word of God, prayer, worship and spirituality, living distinctively Christian lives, sharing resources with the local and wider faith community, responsibility for mutual spiritual development, good stewardship of resources and, very importantly, a willingness to share the Good News in all its dimensions with others. Parents and guardians have, as the primary educators of their children, special responsibilities in each of these areas. They are called to exercise great care in fostering the faith within the social and cultural environment in which they live; and with tremendous care and gentleness to ensure that their children develop the knowledge and skills which will enable them to make responsible sound moral and ethical decisions in life.

- What are you doing now to prepare the next generation of young Catholics for the days when Sunday Mass and the Sacraments will not be as available to us and to them?

- How are the seven elements of church given life in your homes?

- What processes have you in place to ensure that your children and those who visit with you have opportunities to experience worship, mission and ministry?

Let us pray

God of all peoples and nations, Dorcas and her companions lived the Spiritual and Corporal Works of Mercy creatively in their time, under the guidance of your Holy Spirit. In our time we long to follow their example and to bring your Gospel to life in a new way; in a way that speaks to the needs and problems of our time. We pray that we may be especially effective in counteracting human trafficking, substance abuse, the proliferation of nuclear weapons and wars. As members of a first world nation, we pray for the grace to act as hospitable hosts to immigrants, transit camp migrants, refugees and displaced persons. We pray especially for women and children who are victims of domestic abuse, kidnap or used for commercial sex and the gratification of the dysfunctional. With Dorcas we make our prayer to you in the name of Jesus and in union with the Holy Spirit. Amen.

NOTES

1   Herbert Lockyer. *All the Women of the Bible.* Zondervan Publications, Grand Rapids, Michigan. 1967. p. 46.
2   Gail R. O'Day. "Acts" in *Women's Bible Commentary,* Eds. Carol A. Newsom and Sharon H. Ringe. Westminster, John Knox Press, Louisville, Kentucky. 1998. p. 396.
3   Herbert Lockyer. *All the Women of the Bible.* Zondervan Publications, Grand Rapids, Michigan. 1967. p. 47.
4   Edited by Raymond E. Brown, SS., Joseph A Fitzmyer, SJ., & Roland E. Murphy, O.Cam. *The New Jerome Biblical Commentary.* Prentice Hall, Englewood Cliffs, New Jersey. 1990, 1968. p. 745.
5   Elizabeth Schüssler Fiorenza, *In Memory of Her: A Feminist Theological Reconstruction of Christian Origins.* Crossroads, New York. 1994. p. 167.

Mary the Mother of John Mark:
Protector, Provider and Proclaimer

He [Peter] went to the house of Mary, the mother of John whose other name was Mark, where many were gathered together and were praying.

Acts 12:12

This story of Peter, Mary and John Mark is set in Jerusalem in about the year 43 AD, during a period of persecution and transition in the life of the early church. Two years previously a new emperor, Claudius, had been appointed in Rome with the support of Herod Agrippa whom he rewarded with the Kingship of Judea and Samaria, reuniting the territory governed by Agrippa's grand father, Herod the Great. The new king was swift in aligning himself with Jewish nationalism, demonstrating that he observed the Law of Moses, courting the favour of the Jews, and demonstrating his determination to deal ruthlessly with the new Christian movement which was expanding beyond Jerusalem and Judea.

By having James, the brother of John killed in 43 AD, Herod delighted the Jews as this confirmed his strong opposition to Christianity. He was determined to terrorise the disciples out of existence. In order to leave the Jewish leaders in no doubt about this ideology, he imprisoned Peter with the intention of having him executed on ·the day after Passover (Acts 12:4). All of this made the Christian

community feel in constant danger. It was obvious to them that they were seen as a threat to the Roman gods and to the authority of the Emperor who saw himself as having 'godly powers'. Anything that was perceived as a hazard to Roman control must be crushed. This had to be done in a way that would scare potential challengers.

Like any oppressed group the post Pentecost disciples were quick to create a network of support and to establish 'safe places'. Mary the Mother of John Mark provided one such location, and Peter, the leader of the community, was amongst the first to take advantage of it.

When Herod Agrippa saw that it pleased the Jews, [to have James killed], he proceeded to arrest Peter also. This was during the days of Unleavened Bread. And when he had seized him, he put him in prison, and delivered him to four squads of soldiers to guard him, intending after the Passover to bring him out to the people… and behold, an angel of the Lord appeared, and a light shone in the cell; and he struck Peter on the side and woke him, saying, "Get up quickly." And the chains fell off his hands. And the angel said to him, "Dress yourself and put on your sandals." And he did so. And he said to him, "Wrap your mantle around you and follow me." And he went out and followed him; he did not know that what was done by the angel was real, but thought he was seeing a vision… And Peter came to himself, and said, "Now I am sure that the Lord has sent his angel and rescued me from the hand of Herod and from all that the Jewish people were expecting."

When he realized this, he went to the house of Mary, the mother of John whose other name was Mark, where many were gathered together and were praying. And when he knocked at the door of the gateway, a maid named Rhoda came to answer. Recognizing Peter's voice, in her joy she did not open the gate but ran in and told them that Peter was standing at the gate.

They said to her, "You are mad." But she insisted that it was so. They said, "It is his angel!" But Peter continued knocking; and when they opened, they saw him and were amazed. But motioning to them with his hand to be silent, he described to them how the Lord had brought him out of the prison. And he said, "Tell this to James and to the brethren." Then he departed and went to another place. Acts 12:3-4; 7-9; 11-17

Mary is thought to have been a disciple of Jesus during the later period of his public ministry and to have hosted some of his gatherings in Jerusalem (Mk 14:13). Her house stood in its own grounds and was well set back from the main street. It is believed to have been situated in the western section of the city not far from the house of the High Priest in Upper Jerusalem[1]. Its architecture and scale would have reflected that of all the elaborate 'upper room' houses in the area occupied by the city's elite. Mary made it a locus for much of the church's activity.[2] Archaeological research has established that 'upper rooms' in Jerusalem were generally large enough to facilitate up to one hundred and twenty or more people.

Scholars believe that Mary came from the Levite priestly family. Excavators have discovered that this family were known to be part of the very rich, bordering on the aristocracy. Their homes stood on the hills and benefited from the fresh bright sunshine and gentle Mediterranean winds. They contrasted sharply with those in the lower city south of the Temple where the residents were the working class, the poor, and mendicants. This area stank from the odours of animal waste, street markets and rotting produce.

Commodious homes such as Mary's in the upper city are said to have been a reflection of the first century Roman villas in the city of Pompeii and to have had tiled roofs and elaborate bathrooms and pluming systems. Such rooms could, as in the story of the raising of the son of the Shunammite woman, be accessed by a stairway from outside (2 Kings 4: 18-36). They would have been equivalent to contemporary reception or conference rooms.

Some modern scholars believe that Mary, a Jewess of the tribe of Levi, was born in Cyprus and that she was an aunt or a first cousin to Barnabas (Acts 4:36) who had also been born on the island.[3] Their families had possibly gone into exile during the last days of the Diaspora. There she married a wealthy fellow member of the Levite family. In time they were blest with the birth of their only son, Mark. His father gave him the Jewish name Yochanan meaning John and the Greek name Markos or Mark. The giving of both names would not have been unusual at that time as illustrated by the story of Tabitha/Dorcas (Acts 9:36). On the death of her husband, Mary, supported by the extended male family, is thought to have sold her property. Like many of her neighbours and relations she returned to her family roots in Jerusalem. There, she and her son are thought to have eventually inherited more property which had been reclaimed earlier by her father and father-in-law.

Within a short time of their return, Mary is thought to have become friends with widows such as Salome through whom she and Mark were introduced to Jesus and the disciples. Luke tells us that Barnabas sold a field which belonged to him, *"and brought the money and laid it at the apostles' feet"* (Acts 4:37b). This illustrates that like his cousin Mary, he had become a wholehearted disciple. At this time the disciples could freely attend worship in both the synagogues and the Temple because Christianity was simply seen as a sect of Nazarenes.[4] However, in time this would change radically and house churches such as Mary's home would become the norm.

Her son John Mark had become friends with Peter and the other disciples. Mary appears to have supported his new friendship circle. So close did Mark become to the twelve and to Jesus that he is thought to be the young man who had his wrap ripped from his body by the mob, when Jesus was arrested in Gethsemane (Mk14:51-52). His commitment to Jesus must have had a profound affect on Mary. It may have been his relationship with the group that finally convinced her to become a disciple. That she became a respected and valued member is made clear by Luke, who made a point of recording her name in his 'history' of the apostles' work. Only women who held distinctive positions in the early church are mentioned in the writings of Luke.

Mary is accounted for as 'the Mother of John

Mark'. This may be explained by the fact that in the androcentric environment in which Jesus and the disciples lived and operated women were generally recognised in terms of their husband, as in Pilate's wife (Mt 27:8-19); their father, as in Jarius' daughter (Lk 8:40-42), or some other male relative, as in the mother of the sons of Zebedee (Mt 20:20).[5] That the house is described as the property of Mary possibly means that when she and Mark first met the disciples, Mark was still a junior. In the years to come he would become a fellow missionary with Barnabas (Acts 15:39), fall foul of Paul (Acts 15:37); be referred to affectionately by Peter as 'my son' (1 Pet 5:13); be reconciled with Paul (Col 4:10); and according to tradition, become father to the church in Alexandria. Mary had a right to be proud of her son. She put both her home and her wealth at the disposal of the new faith community. Scholars are divided as to whether it was in her house that Jesus shared the Last Supper with the disciples. Many believe and probably rightly so that it was. Jesus certainly knew the house and its owner before sending the two disciples there to request that it be prepared in traditional Jewish style for the sacred celebration of the Passover:

And on the first day of Unleavened Bread, when they sacrificed the Passover lamb, his disciples said to him, "Where will you have us go and prepare for you to eat the Passover?" And he sent two of his disciples, and said to them, "Go into the city, and a man carrying a jar of water will meet you; follow him, and wherever he enters, say to the householder, 'The Teacher says, Where is my guest room, where

I am to eat the Passover with my disciples?' And he will show you a large upper room furnished and ready; there prepare for us."   Mk 14:13-26

It is not surprising that he chose to share his last festive meal there before his passion. It is a wonderful tribute to Mary's hospitality and reverence that it was probably in her 'upper room' that he instituted the Eucharist in the presence of the wider discipleship. There he commissioned the entire gathering to: "*Do this in remembrance of me*" (Lk 22:19b). A new covenant was being inaugurated. Mary as host, together with the entire discipleship who had come up from Galilee, were to be the witnesses. They were to take responsibility for enabling it to be renewed and celebrated in "the breaking of bread", amongst the wider and ever growing community in the days when Jesus was no longer with them (Acts 20:7; 1 Cor 10:16,17; 11:23-26).

Mary's involvement with the emerging church appears to have become very much more intense and unconditional following the Pentecost experience. Initially it was relatively easy to be part of the discipleship and to support through hospitality and prayer. However, once Herod Agrippa made his presence felt and his agenda clear, unconditional commitment became a risky and dangerous pledge. Despite this, Mary was willing to take risks because she firmly believed in what she was doing. She understood the need for holistic living, sanctification, compassion and for liberation from some of the rigid, inhuman and restrictive Jewish rules, such as:

> *"...If any harm follows, then you shall give life for life, eye for eye, tooth for tooth, hand for hand, foot for foot, burn for burn, wound for wound, stripe for stripe."*   Ex 21:23-25

And again:

> *"He who kills a beast shall make it good, life for life. When a man causes a disfigurement in his neighbour, as he has done it shall be done to him, fracture for fracture, eye for eye, tooth for tooth; as he has disfigured a man, he shall be disfigured."*
> Lev 24:18-20

Mary made clear to the faith community that she was willing to take risks for the Gospel, and that there was always a place for them in her home.

The fact that Peter knew he could come to Mary's house and be assured of a joyful welcome following his miraculous escape from prison speaks volumes for her steadfastness, courage, hospitality and availability. Knowing that the disciples had taken Jesus' instructions on the prayer of supplication seriously, he also knew that he would find the community assembled in payer (Mt 18:19; Mt 21:22; Mk 11:24; Jn 14:13-14). He had been incarcerated in the Antonia Fortress about half a mile from Mary's house. Like all houses of its style, Mary's had the protection of a courtyard, large gate and a strong and firmly locked door. Hers was a quiet, very secure and safe space that could not easily be interrupted or accessed. She was fortunate enough to be able to afford the services of a maid, Rhoda, who also acted as door-keeper.

When Peter arrived at the gate frightened and in

shock, he knocked loudly, fiercely and consistently, calling out his name as he did so, in keeping with local requirements. Rhoda heard Peter's voice but instead of running to his rescue, she was overcome with joy, and ran to the assembled community to announce the good news. As Luke tells us, they thought that she had become deranged (Acts 12:15). She was not the first woman in the New Testament to have her word doubted by an assembled male community.

On the occasion of the Resurrection, the women who brought the news to the eleven, were written off as the carriers of idle tales (Lk 24:1-11).[6] Ten to twelve years on, the dominant androcentric view of women had not changed, not even in the Christian community, it seems. Rhoda, being a maid and the doorkeeper had far less credibility than the women who returned from the tomb. However, she got the same treatment which demonstrated that no woman's word was accepted as credible unless it was verified and that preferably by a man.

While the community argued amongst themselves, Peter kept on calling and knocking. A visit from him would have been a source of immense delight not only to the excitable teenage doorkeeper, Rhoda, but to the entire recently Christianised family. Eventually they opened the gate and discovered to their great joy and surprise that it was Peter. Fearing that Herod's guards and soldiers might discover him, and having greeted Mary and the disciples; he instructed them to let James, who was to become the first bishop of Jerusalem, know that he was safe. Then he disappeared into the night streets as suddenly as he had appeared at Mary's gate.

The following morning after an investigation, Herod had Peter's guards put to death (Acts 12:19). This demonstrated the depth of cruelty to which he was willing to stoop. Nobody knows where Peter went for safety until after Herod's unexpected death in 44 AD. "Divine custody of the apostle and vengeance against the persecutor are the exquisite counterpoints of this section"[7] [of Luke's history]. Peter next appears in Acts chairing the Council of Jerusalem in 49 AD.

In relating this story of Mary's hospitality, Luke presents two women, Mary and Rhoda in a positive light. However, he places it firmly in the period of Peter's ministry. As with the story of Dorcas, his intention is not so much to affirm wonderful women in ministry as it is to show the miraculous intervention of God in support of Peter.[8] It is also directed at portraying him as leader and as the persistent and irrestrainable proclaimer of the Good News. However, it does depict each woman as having a distinct contribution to make to both witness and proclamation. Each is shown to have carried out her ministry with joy and enthusiasm.

This was not Peter's first encounter with a female servant and doorkeeper. During Jesus' Passion, he had been confronted by both the doorkeeper and the fire-stoker in the palace of the courtyard of the High Priest. On that occasion he had served his master less than well, while they had been perceptive and dutiful. They had put the interests of their master above the comfort of one who had a right to avail of the comforts of the fire while he awaited a decision on his master's future (Mk 14:66-72).

In this circumstance he was trying to enter 'the

house of his Lord', the place where the new church had so often gathered with Mary, and in his presence, for prayer and for the breaking of bread. The joy of Rhoda contrasts sharply on this occasion with the remorse of Peter as he left the courtyard of the High Priest weeping bitterly because of the guilt he felt at having denied his Master (Lk 22:62). Jesus had rescued him then and would do likewise now. Then he felt crushed. Now he felt liberated. Like Mary, and the entire assembly, he was grateful and determined to continue to journey with the Holy Spirit in order to bring the Good News of salvation to all nations (Mt 28:19).

Mary was one of the key women supporting the male disciples during this period of persecution and transition from synagogue to house churches, from Judea to Antioch, Cyprus and Rome. That Rhoda recognised Peter's voice and felt free to interrupt the assembly shows that Mary made her servants feel very much part of the family and at home. This contrasts with how servants were treated in the households of the elite at that time. It demonstrates that the teaching of Jesus was not just an admired or preached theory. It was rather a lived reality. The network of protection and safety extended to the male disciples was given life and heart in all Mary's domestic relationships. The rights and dignity of staff were respected. Mary's household was truly a 'safe place' for all, who, motivated by the Holy Spirit, lived by and promoted the Good News of Jesus, the Saviour.

Reflection

Soon after Pentecost, the Christians became an oppressed community very quickly. This forced them to rethink their mission status in Jerusalem, and to put a safety strategy in place. It is interesting that they did not return violence for violence. Their Pentecost faith and openness to discerning the ways of the Holy Spirit had grown even stronger in the passing ten years. Once again the women disciples such as Mary the Mother of John Mark came to the rescue, and like the women of Jerusalem, they never thought of their own security and safety (Lk 23: 27-31).

They had made a commitment to witness and proclamation. They would carry out that ministry under the guidance of the Holy Spirit making use of all resources available to them. In times of serious, planned and organised persecution they discerned that the best way they could witness was through converting their homes into: 'safe places' and feeding stations for the hunted; house-churches for prayer groups, faith sharing, evangelisation and the 'breaking of bread'; work and craft centres for women to make clothes and food for the poor; distribution centres for goods collected for mendicants and the disposed; and hospitality centres for returning missionaries who needed rest and renewal. In these ways they became the core and heart of the ever expanding faith community.

Mary, Rhoda and their sisters made the Beatitudes their own (Mt 5:2-11). They were certainly the poor in spirit who quickly learned from their male colleagues what real practical and physical poverty was like when 'on the run' daily. The men had been forced to depend on women such as Mary for sustenance, to find a different place to sleep each night and to be ready to run for cover at a moment's notice.

- According to *Pax Christi*, our UK government used about £29bn on military expenditure in 2005. It plans to renew trident and to ensure nuclear security into the foreseeable future. What does that tell us about the attitude of our so-called Christian Leadership to violence/non-violence?

- What is our attitude to peace/violence as Christian citizens of a world where twelve times as much money is spent on war as on third world aid?

- In our day the Parish Church stands as the centre of community life and worship. Are there any identifiable similarities between its ethos of care, evangelisation, protection of the vulnerable, 'hunted' as in refugees and victims of injustice when compared with the ambience in the house of Mary?

- How are the members of your parish community encouraged and helped to live lives that speak of Pentecost to others?

- Is faith sharing an integral part of parish programmes today or is it left to the priest, and maybe religious sisters, to bring small groups together on special occasions for such on-going evangelisation practices?

Mary and her sisters were the merciful who were there to show mercy to others while being denied it

themselves by soldiers and guards who, without warning or permission, broke into their homes in search of members of the twelve. They were the ones who comforted the sorrowful and sent pleas to men such as Peter to '*raise the dead*' (Acts 9:40). They were the pure in heart who saw God at work in everything and who ensured that there was food available for the seven deacons to distribute to poor widows, orphans and mendicants, while often going hungry themselves (6:3).

- To what extent do our parishes engage in the Corporal Works of Mercy in an organised way?

- How might we help to make modern families more aware of the Christian need for young people to make a definite commitment to the Spiritual and Corporal Works of Mercy today?

Mary and her sisters in faith were the persecuted as they strove to ensure that the male disciples were free to answer calls to evangelise and to baptise (Acts 10:34-43). They were amongst those who were reviled, and about whom evil was spoken through jealousy (6:5-15). Instead of adopting the Jewish maxim of an eye for an eye, it could be rightly said of them that they, like Jesus, forgave their tormentors knowing that they acted out of ignorance (Lk 23:34).

- Who are the merciful, poor, persecuted, peace-makers, pure in heart, meek, mourners, and hungry; both spiritually and materially in your neighbourhoods today?

So precious and sacred has the memory of Mary and the many sacred meetings and services held in her house by both Jesus and the apostles become that Christians down through history feel a need to cling to it. Many believe and, indeed state as fact, that it stood on the site currently occupied by the Cenacle in Jerusalem. While archaeologists keep an open mind on this, it is thought that the original site cannot be identified with historical authenticity.

Since the home and all relating to it was the domain of women and since Luke takes their presence in ministry in the emerging church, for granted, it is most likely that many, many women fulfilled roles in a variety of essential ministries under the broad umbrellas of the Beatitudes (Mt 5:2-11), and the Corporal Works of Mercy (Mt 25:35-45).

As Mary Ann Getty Sullivan points out, women acted alone and in partnership with others.[2] They were widows, people of influence, women who were domestic aids such as Rhoda, and women who gave support on a part-time basis. In many cases they were the residential faithful who prepared food including the bread and wine for the 'breaking of bread' ritual. They testified to the Resurrection and the presence of the Holy Spirit. In short, the very survival of the church depended on them.

In an address entitled "Discipleship for a Priestly People in Priestless Time", delivered to a Conference on Women's Ordination in Dublin, the well known Benedictine Sister, Joan Chittister, spoke about the meaning of discipleship in the early church. She pointed out that to be a Christian meant having to defy Roman Imperialism, to stretch Judaism and to counteract pagan values. It called for rejection of emperor worship, rejection of animal sacrifices and the inhumane aspects of the Law. It welcomed the inclusion of women, the Gentiles and the replacement of nationalism with universalism. It is fair to say that the challenges of discipleship in our day are no less. We face a new imperialism, and we are called to be to our time what Jesus, Mary, Rhoda and the twelve were to theirs. We are summoned to be Jesus in our day, to be Eucharist to our parish communities, our area, nation and world. In our media driven world, we are called upon to be global Christians.

- At a time when we are experiencing a severe shortage of priests in active ministry, might it be possible that the Holy Spirit is inviting us to reflect once more on the model of house-churches run by Mary and the other holy women?

Maybe the Holy Spirit is using this time of apparent famine as a means of inviting us to reflect on new models of priesthood and new ways of being parish. Jesus, the original priest, left us in no doubt that we are his human agents in our world. Like him we have a transforming ministry to fulfil. As American President Theodore Roosevelt told his people in his Inaugural Speech in March 1905, God calls on each one of us to leave at least one little bit of our world a better place socially, spiritually and physically when we leave it, than it was when we entered it.

The concept of Basic Christian Community (A Plan for Restructuring the Parish and Renewal of Catholic Life[9]), as promoted by Fr Arthur R. Baranowski of Michigan, has done much to give new life to Catholics in various areas of the United States. As Baranowski points out, the lifestyle asked of the disciple by Christ and by the church demands a conversion of life based on daily reflection.

- How many parishes provide creative plans for bringing people together in ways that constantly support the people in their struggle to live the gospel in our post modern and post Christian age?

The three key ingredients of the house-church and of Basic Christian Communities (satellites of the main parish) were and are: experience of loving social, spiritual and moral life-giving support; communal prayer incorporating 'the breaking of bread'; and enthusiasm for the faith and proclamation.

- How life-giving are the majority of our parishes today?

- Do parishes organise small groups in which women and men together can share faith and welcome new members to their streets, roads or area?

- Does the way we incorporate new members into our church and engage with them in ministry speak of the reality of our parish life?

- What might need to be changed in our parishes or models of priesthood to renew the life of our faith communities?

- Might the inclusion of women in the Upper Room on Pentecost Sunday, and in ministry in the early

church, have any message for us today in terms of ministry and priesthood?

Let us pray

Gracious God, we thank you for giving us Mary the mother of John Mark as the paradigm of all the wonderfully Spirit-filled, compassionate, hospitable and caring mothers who have preceded us in faith. We pray that by following in their footsteps and allowing the Holy Spirit to direct our lives we will imitate their courage and fidelity. We ask your intercession as we say:

Spirit of God and hospitality of Mary,
    have mercy on us
Compassion of God and protector of Peter,
    have mercy on us
Joy and enthusiasm in the person of Rhoda,
    have mercy on us
Seeker of justice for all peoples, races and nations,
    have mercy on us
Giver of hope to all women and men who are widowed,
    have mercy on us.

Companion to women in times of fear and uncertainty,
    be our strength
Lover of refugees, the homeless poor and the oppressed,
    be our strength
Healer of the broken, imprisoned and threatened,
    be our strength
Healer of the violated, mentally abused and bullied,
    be our strength
Victim of injustice, be our strength
Companion to the wounded, targeted, hunted and
    abandoned, be our strength.

Tenderness of God, be our receptionist
Worker of Wonders, be our receptionist
Advocate of women, be our receptionist
Friend to missionaries, be our receptionist
Doorkeeper to the Paschal Banquet,
    be our receptionist.

We make this prayer through Jesus Christ our model
    and Saviour. Amen.

NOTES

1   Joanne Turpin. *Twelve Apostolic Women*. St Anthony Messenger Press, Cincinnati, Ohio. 2004. p. 56.

2   Mary Anne Getty-Sullivan. *Women in the New Testament*. The Liturgical Press, Collegeville, Minnesota. 2001. p. 234-235.

3   Herbert Lockyer. *All the Women of the Bible*. Zondervan Publications, Grand Rapids, Michigan. 1967. p. 107.

4   Brien E. Shafer. "In A Mother's House". Sermon Archive. Internet Publication 2006.

5   Kathleen Murphy. *The Women of the Passion*. St Pauls Publications, London. 2005. p. 42.

6   Gail R. O'Day. "Acts" in *Women's Bible Commentary*, Eds. Carol A. Newsom and Sharon H Ringe. Westminster John Knox Press, Louisville, Kentucky. 1998. p. 399.

7   Edited by Raymond E. Brown, SS., Joseph A Fitzmyer, SJ., & Roland E. Murphy, O.Cam. *The New Jerome Biblical Commentary*. Prentice Hall, Englewood Cliffs, New Jersey. 1990, 1968. p. 747.

8   Clarice J. Martin. The Acts of the Apostles in *Searching the Scriptures* Vol 2. Ed. Elizabeth Schüssler Fiorenza. Crossroads Publ., New York. 1994. p. 782.

9   Arthur R. Baranowski. *Creating Small Faith Communities: A Plan for Restructuring the Parish and Renewing Catholic Life*. St Anthony Messenger Press, Cincinnati. 1988.

Lydia: Convert, Communicator and Collaborator

And when she was baptized, with her household, she besought us, saying, "If you have judged me to be faithful to the Lord, come to my house and stay." And she prevailed upon us. Acts 16:15

Luke's use of the word 'us', here indicates that he was an eye witness to the conversion of Lydia. He had journeyed with Paul and Silas to Philippi, modern Kavalla, and observed four key events in which the Gentile woman Lydia, became not only the first of Paul's converts in the city, but also the first European female to embrace Christianity and become a collaborator with the apostles in mission.[1]

Scholars believe that Lydia, meaning Lydian woman, came originally, from the province of Lydia in Asia Minor, modern Turkey, which had been conquered by Rome in 133 BC. It was a rich province and ruled over by a governor with the title of proconsul. It had been a popular settlement for Jewish entrepreneurs. Judaism had attracted many Gentile women because of its worship, high ethical practices and moral principles.

Lydia would have been one of the many slave women who were enriched by the faith but had not made a commitment to it. She would have learned the delicate skills of mixing dyes and selecting materials of the finest texture in order to facilitate the needs of Jewish temple worship (Ex 25-28, 35,36,38-39), as well as royalty and the elite in society through the entire region and beyond. Purple cloth continued to be a luxury item for both genders amongst the rich and famous in New Testament times as illustrated by Luke: *"There was a rich man, who was clothed in purple and fine linen…"* (16:19).

On gaining her freedom, she continued her study with a firm in the city of Thyatira, a city devoted to the pagan god Apollo who was worshipped as the sun-god under the name Tyrinnus.[2] Freedom could be won either by labouring assiduously for it, or by buying it outright. Tyrinnus was a cosmopolitan city situated about forty miles inland across the Aegean Sea from Athens. Having made her name as a skilled and discerning dyer, Lydia emigrated to Philippi in Macedonia.

There having, while still a slave, gained knowledge of the needs and expensive tastes of the rich and famous, she set up her own business. "Artisans there had developed a method of making a purple dye from the madder root – an alternative to the more costly dye derived from the rare murex shellfish in Phoenician waters."[3] Lydia probably held many secrets about the mixing of colours, and methods of creating the most exquisite red and scarlet dyes from a grub nurtured on special trees such as the oak. Other precious sources were the turmeric, sunflower and the peel of the pomegranate. Lydia was an entrepreneur and a proud professional. She was probably seen as an adviser and buyer in a flourishing international and commercial trade.

Her training and the relationship which she had

formed with traders while still in the dyers guild in Thyatira enabled her to make rapid economic progress in her new home and to establish easy relationships with the locals. Jewish women would have been delighted with her services; her commitment to their prayer group and her stories about her travels as a trader. Her poise, skills and modest dignity would have endeared her to them. Many would have viewed her as a role model. She would have been a good and ethical employer to her slaves and to all those whom she engaged to support and lead her business.

Philippi was *the leading city of the district of Macedo'nia* (Acts 16:12), and an ideal situation for an enterprising, skilled and ambitious trader. Twentieth century excavations have shown that it had its own forum, agora, public baths, theatre, gymnasium, temple and shrines to a variety of deities. Like the colony of Lydia in Asia Minor in which Lydia had been born and learned her trade, Philippi, as part of Macedonia, was governed by Rome. It was bisected by the famous Via Egnalia highway which made it a prized centre and route for merchants and traders. Rome's control of Philippi would serve Paul well during his more difficult evangelising days in the city. When Lydia met Paul, Silas and Luke there, she had a basic understanding of monotheism, the value of prayer and knowledge of the Promise made to Abraham (Gen 17:1-16).

She was a seeker of truth, not just in the dye and fine materials trade, but in her search for the meaning and the purpose of life. In short she was searching for the salvation that can only be found in Jesus. She had met all kinds of people, religious sects and philosophical ideas during her travels. Luke does not tell us what Paul said in his address that influenced Lydia. But we can be sure that he proclaimed salvation through Jesus Christ the Promised One of God; and spoke about his teachings, miracles, death and resurrection and his gift of the Holy Spirit to the church. So impressed was Lydia by what she heard that she not only asked for baptism for herself but was instrumental in getting her entire household to join her in the commitment:

> One who heard us was a woman named Lydia, from the city of Thyati'ra, a seller of purple goods, who was a worshiper of God. The Lord opened her heart to give heed to what was said by Paul. And when she was baptized, with her household, she besought us, saying, "If you have judged me to be faithful to the Lord, come to my house and stay." And she prevailed upon us.   Acts 16:15

Household in this context would have included all her slaves, her employees and some of her business partners who lived with and close to her. Lydia and her household became an island of Christian life in an unbelieving world.[4] Her hospitality is reflective of that of Cornelius who having been baptised by Peter shared his new-found faith with his entire household (Acts 10:1-11:18). Both stories combine to show the holistic goodness and hospitality of women and men alike when it came to sharing the faith in the early church. Lydia's contribution to "leadership is portrayed in terms of a benefactor who provides resources and hospitality for those under whose leadership the mission will develop."[5]

She did not hold the position of deacon herself; nor did she downsize her business. Rather, as a woman fired with the energy of Pentecost, she had the vision to inspire other women such as Euodia and Syntyche in leadership (Phil 1:4). As a committed member of the community, and when her work schedule allowed, she would have spent some time each week in ministry to deprived and socially disadvantaged members of the community. This would entail visiting the sick and imprisoned, giving alms to the needy and, educating enquirers about the life, death and resurrection of Jesus.[6] It would have been a priority to ensure that everyone knew that Jesus was the fulfilment of the Promise and that Salvation was a gift through him.

In addition to this and as mistress of the house she would have led prayers and shared in the breaking of bread with the new community celebrating in her home. Paul made a remarkable impression on the group and so endeared himself to the people that Philippi would ever remain one of his favourite churches (Phil 1:2-5). Lydia is not unlike Mary, the Mother of John Mark, who had property, wealth and the acumen to bring others with her to Jesus; and to designate her home as a safe place and the first house-church on European soil.

Luke portrays women as home-makers, carers and providers of hospitality in both his Gospel (Lk 1:56; 17:35; 23:27,55), and again in Acts, *"If you have judged me to be faithful to the Lord, come to my house and stay"* (Acts 16:15). The missionaries were happy to accept the invitation and to make the house their first Christian foundation in Macedonia.

Luke proceeds to introduce the second of the four

key events relating to Paul's time as guest of Lydia:

> *As we were going to the place of prayer, we were met by a slave girl who had a spirit of divination and brought her owners much gain by soothsaying. She followed Paul and us, crying, "These men are servants of the Most High God, who proclaim to you the way of salvation." And this she did for many days. But Paul was annoyed, and turned and said to the spirit, "I charge you in the name of Jesus Christ to come out of her." And it came out that very hour.* Acts 16:16-18

Here Luke is telling the story of another female who was marginalised fourfold, "according to traditional androcentric and patriarchal norms, by virtue of her gender (woman), status (slave), her possession by a spirit of divination, and her economic exploitation (exploited by her owners as a fortune-teller).[7] This is the only reference in Acts to a female being possessed by and healed from a demon or evil spirit. Interestingly of the eleven references to possession in the Synoptic Gospels only three refer to the female gender: the healing of a woman *who had a spirit of infirmity*, on the Sabbath (Lk 13:11-17); the healing of a Canaanite woman's daughter who had been *severely possessed by a demon* (Mt 15:22-29; Mk 7: 25-30). This is the first recorded exorcism carried out by Paul.

The woman's words and behaviour toward the missionaries reflects that of the Canaanite woman whose daughter Jesus healed, in that both women recognised the goodness, work and power of God in human agents before they experienced it for themselves. I refer to Jesus here as human in the sense that while he was on earth, his miraculous power came from God rather than from using his divine giftedness while still living out his humanity. His initial response to the woman was: *"I was sent only to the lost sheep of the house of Israel"* (Mt 15:24), indicating that he was carrying out a mission on behalf of a higher power meaning God. Likewise, in his healing of the crippled woman, Jesus *"laid his hands upon her, and immediately she was made straight, and she praised God"* (Lk 13:13). The laying on of hands signified the calling down of the Holy Spirit. So here, too, the human Jesus was not relying on his own authority but on that of God as praised by the woman.

Paul on the other hand commanded: *"I charge you in the name of Jesus Christ to come out of her"* (Acts 16:18). He recognised that of himself he had no power but was working through that of Jesus who had now transcended the human state and was working out of oneness with God. The drama of this story is mildly reminiscent of that surrounding Jesus' healing of the crippled woman on the Sabbath (Lk 13:14-15). The leader of the synagogue was enraged and so were the owners of this unfortunate woman.

Both the motivation for the healing and the reason for the violent reactions were, of course, different in each case. Jesus acted out of compassion: *"And ought not this woman, a daughter of Abraham whom Satan bound for eighteen years, be loosed from this bond on the Sabbath day?"* (13:16); while Paul appears to have acted out of frustration. Frustration because of the way the woman kept pursuing his party: *"These men are servants of the Most High God, who proclaim to you the way of salvation"* (Acts 16:20), coupled with the fact that she was being abused and exploited by her owners as a fortune teller.

This young woman stands in sharp contrast to Lydia, to whom she was a challenge. She was also a challenge to many people in Philippi in the sense that she was proclaiming a demanding truth. She recognised Paul and Silas as *"servants of the Most High God, who proclaim to you the way of salvation"* (16:17). Some women scholars wonder if in leaving the woman at the point where Paul silenced her demon, instead of moving on to tell of her conversion to Christianity, Luke is demonstrating his personal discomfort with the idea of women having a prophetic voice in the church.[8]

This is certainly not the case because he goes on to explain that Paul not only silenced her demon but exorcised her as well: *"I charge you in the name of Jesus Christ to come out of her"* (16:10). She had already recognised God at work in Paul and scholars are generally happy to agree that the she joined Lydia as an integral part of her house church. Instead of having just one strong woman to support the emerging church, Philippi was now, blest with two. The narrative also serves to alert Christians to the dangers of the demon resident in mantic arts and the evils of fortune-telling.

Meanwhile Lydia, working like Mary the Mother of Jesus after Pentecost, made it her special ministry to offer hospitality to the apostles. This kindness enabled them to carry on their evangelising activities in a relaxed environment. The miracle of Paul further rooted and extended the church in Philippi and attracted new members locally. However, on hearing the news of the women's conversion, her owners, realising that their source of income had been terminated reacted angrily as Luke proceeds to relate:

> *... they seized Paul and Silas and dragged them into the market place before the rulers; and when they had brought them to the magistrates they said, "These men are Jews and they are disturbing our city. They advocate customs which it is not lawful for us Romans to accept or practice."*
>
> *The crowd joined in attacking them; and the magistrates tore the garments off them and gave orders to beat them with rods. And when they had inflicted many blows upon them, they threw them into prison, charging the jailer to keep them safely. Having received this charge, he put them into the inner prison and fastened their feet in the stocks. But about midnight Paul and Silas were praying and singing hymns to God, and the prisoners were listening to them, And suddenly there was a great earthquake, so that the foundations of the prison were shaken; and immediately all the doors were opened and every one's fetters were unfastened. When the jailer woke and saw that the prison doors were open, he drew his sword and was about to kill himself, supposing that the prisoners had escaped. But Paul cried with a loud voice, "Do not harm yourself, for we are all here."*
>
> Acts 16:19-28

In their rage they made a false charge against Paul and Silas, saying that they were Jews, thus using to their own advantage Roman anti-Jewish feelings. In addition to this they accused them of disturbing the peace of the city, which meant undermining the authority of Rome. This latter accusation was serious. But it was a false charge since Christianity neither detracted from the human honour due to the Emperor nor adversely affected public order. The apostles were incarcerated preparing the way for a third key event in the Paul and Lydia story (16:19-26). An unexpected thunderstorm during the night opened the way for their miraculous release. However, they stood firm realising that they had a mission to the jailer and that as a Roman citizen, Paul had rights of which he had been unjustly deprived.

Meanwhile the jailer panicked thinking that his prisoners had escaped and that he would be held to account for what would appear to be a very serious failure in his stewardship. Paul reassured him that they were present and that his future was secure. What was to follow made the silencing of the 'clairvoyant' pale into oblivion on a temporary basis. The jailer asked Paul for guidance and Paul told him about Jesus and invited him to join the church. *"And he took them the same hour of the night, and washed their wounds, and he was baptized at once, with all his family"* (16:33). Some scholars argue that this was the real "deliverance miracle" in the story of Lydia and the faith of Philippi.[9] From now on, she had the additional support of a man of substance, and a considerably enlarged and consolidated community to work with in Philippi. The hospitality offered by the jailer symbolised the 'breaking of bread' by Jesus in the Upper Room on Passover night and served as a sign that salvation had come to the entire household.

The following morning the magistrates decided to free them. Paul rejected the offer saying that as a Roman citizen he should not have been either flogged or imprisoned without a trial. He proceeded to demand an apology and a dignified escort from the prison (16:35-37). The magistrate immediately vindicated him and freed him with his companions, leading them to the city gates. However, Paul continued to exert his rights and took time with his companions to visit with Lydia, affirm her in her new role, and give his blessing to the growing faith community,[10] *"and when they had seen the brethren, they exhorted them and departed"* (16:40). This vindication is the fourth key point in the story. It is important for a number of reasons most particularly because it demonstrated that giving life to the Gospel through the Corporal Works of Mercy is not a political activity. It is, rather, the deliverance and liberation of God's people from the sins of greed, control, divination, metaphorical imprisonment, abuse and mercenary gain.

The jailer's initial approach to Paul was with a view to saving his own skin, job and lifestyle. Paul gave him the gift of all three. But more importantly, and as he had done for Lydia, he gave him the priceless gift of salvation through baptism in the name of Jesus. In contrast to the jailer, Lydia had been 'a seeker' of truth for some years. Her request to Paul was a purely Spirit centred one, and her outreach in hospitality was truly altruistic. As the first Christian female convert in a European setting, she stands as a beacon to all Christian women who struggle to turn the tide for our diminishing church in the first decade of this third millennium.

The Holy Spirit, who had touched so many hearts in Jerusalem on Pentecost Sunday, now touched the heart of Lydia. She had been preparing herself for the great moment. As St John Chrysostom once said, "To open is the part of God and to pay attention that of the woman." In true Christian fashion as soon as Lydia accepted the faith she reached out in hospitality firstly to her evangelisers and then to the growing faith community. As a confident, well known and respected business woman, she had an extensive property and secure finances. Added to all of these she was blest with the graciousness, availability and detachment that were characteristics of Jesus and that became the distinguishing marks of the faith community.

Lydia was able to see beyond the transient in life to the ultimate and the everlasting. Her years of service from that of slave to free woman, from employee to employer and from travelling as a trader and agent between Asia and Europe, had taught her that there is more to life than status, property, money and power. It had also taught her that it is not the having of property and possessions that is important; or in gospel terms wrong, so much as the use to which they are put. They must always be seen as gifts from God and intended to be used for the enrichment of humanity.

Lydia understood this teaching and lived as Good News amongst her people. She is portrayed as the ideal home-maker. Her centre was her home; and it was there that she insisted on entertaining the missionaries who brought the message of Jesus to her. At her invitation, it was there, too, that Paul established the first house-church in Philippi. Within days he affirmed the concept further by establishing one in the house of the jailer. It should be no surprise to us then that the family is referred to in *Lumen Gentium* (The Dogmatic Constitution on the Church), as the domestic Church, [where] the parents, by word and example, are the first heralds of the faith with regard to their children. They must foster the vocation which is proper to each child, and this with special care if it be to religion."[11]

On 7 February 2007, our Holy Father, Pope Benedict XVI, speaking in his weekly address to all those who assemble in St Peter's Square in Rome, on the theme of 'Witnesses to the Christian Faith', said of the family home:

> "... every home can transform itself into a little church. Not only in the sense that in them must reign the typical Christian love made of altruism and of reciprocal care, but still more in the sense that the whole family life, based on faith, is called to revolve around the singular lordship of Jesus Christ.
>
> Not by chance does Paul compare, in the Letter to the Ephesians, the matrimonial relationship to the spousal communion that happens between Christ and the Church (cf. Eph 5:25-33). Even more, we can maintain that the Apostle indirectly models the life of the entire Church, on that of the family. And the Church, in reality, is the family of God."

- What significance might the fact that a woman was the first named post Pentecost convert in Europe, and that she made her home a house church have for women in this first decade of the third millennium?

- Has the life and life-style of Lydia any message for women at this time when commitment to the faith seems to be diminishing or to be over-shadowed by an apparent attitude of self suff-iciency, climbing the social ladder, glamour and the new god, football?

Frequently business people become so pre-occupied with contracts, markets, international travel and strategies for expansion that they forget their own need for sustenance. The inner person has to be nurtured. The soul must be nourished if the heart, mind and entire body are to function properly. Relationships have to be fostered and cultivated if we are to have the strength and power to transcend our demons, act justly, love tenderly and walk humbly with our God who is Caring Friend, Loving Guide and Merciful Compassion (Mic 6:8). Lydia had taken time to understand these truths. When she found Jesus, she treasured her discovery and encouraged others to join her in spreading the Good News.

We are called to be honourable in business, to be diligent for all that is good and to have a heart for others. God places no premium on shadiness, idleness or on self-centred protectionism. Knowing all the hazard of caring and all the bends in the river of relationships demands from us simply that we love with greater depth and serve with greater generosity. Those who do not know love, forgiveness and compassion become dysfunctional and lonely. Frequently they live some distance from the self-possessed image they project to the world. But their body language, and from time to time, their angry words betray their self imposed deep mental pains of jealousy, frustration and their crushed spirits.

- How can knowing that it is God who opens hearts help home based missionaries in our seemingly post Christian world?

- Hospitality was Lydia's key contribution to the Gospel and the new church. How might we offer a form of hospitality today that might enrich our local faith community and especially our young people?

Lydia came from the margins. She understood the position and social situation of the girl who had become socially, spiritually, emotionally and psychologically detached from her community. To the apostles who brought peace, security and safety to the girl, Lydia provided the water for Baptism. At another level, she became both the healing waters that flow out from Temple and the tree of life – the cross from which the blood of Eucharist and the waters of salvation flowed; firstly for the girl and secondly for the growing faith community in Philippi.

In our days women face a new form of marginalisation and slavery created by greedy, dysfunctional and unprincipled men who traffic and trade women and girls for prostitution. Victims are subjected to coercion, beatings, fraud and sexual exploitation. Between 600,000 to 800,000 innocent victims are trafficked through international borders annually. Approximately 14,500 to 17,500 are taken to the USA. Up to 20,000 have been trafficked into the UK. While it is difficult to get any realistic figures for Ireland, statistics in the public domain indicate that about two hundred women have been trafficked from countries such as Lithuania, Russia, Albania, Ukraine, Malaysia, Thailand, the People's Republic of China, East and Central Africa, Nigeria, and Ghana in recent times. The reality is probably very different from and well in excess of this.

Frequently women and children are told that jobs await them in the restaurant and hotel industry. Some women come ready to accept immoral employment as lap dancers and escorts. But most do not know that prostitution is all that awaits them. They are our third millennium slaves and some are only twelve years old. Despite this, they are forced into prostitution, sexual pornography, sexual tourism and child labour.

In response to this pernicious social crime, the Sisters of Mercy opened a rescue day centre, 'Women at the Well', in London on the Feast of Our Lady of Mercy, 24 September 2007. Founded on Gospel values, the centre aims to direct all energies into providing a creative and supportive space where these vulnerable women will receive an holistic response to their needs. The Mercy Sisters' hope is that the help they, and their co-workers, give to these women in developing new skills, will enable them to make choices which will improve the quality of their lives and provide them with possibilities for meaningful and life-giving employment. What a wonderfully Christian way of 'breaking bread' with women and girls who are dehumanised by mercenary gangs, and who like the girl suffering from divination at Philippi, need to be liberated and rehabilitated.

Shortly after the Sisters had the vision to start this pioneering centre, the British Government launched 'Operation Pentameter 2'. The specific aims of which is to: identify and disrupt all those criminals involved in human trafficking, rescue innocent victims, acquaint the community at large with the problems of trafficking, heighten knowledge and understanding of this new form of criminality, and demonstrate that the United Kingdom is hostile ground for criminals who engage in this new form of slavery.

- Who are the marginalised in your area? Are there any organised forms of support available to these children of God?

- What processes are in place in your community to welcome back those, who for whatever reason, were once marginalised?

- Are the rehabilitated enabled, invited or allowed, like Lydia and the freed girl at Philippi, to use their academic, employment and leadership skills in the service of the economy and the faith community?

- Is there anyway in which you or your parish can reach out to alleviate human trafficking or contemporary female and child slavery?

- How might Lydia's search for the Gospel and giving of her home as a meeting place for the local church help women, men and young people today who long for friendship, wholeness and spiritual nourishment?

Let us pray

God of all peoples and nations, we praise you for giving us Lydia as the first European woman to accept faith in Jesus. Thank you for granting her the grace never to lose the life of the Holy Spirit implanted in her heart at the moment of her conception, despite the challenges she faced on her journey from child-slave to free woman; from student to teacher; from employee to employer; from doing business with kings, designers and the elite in the society of her day, to seeking you in prayer in the simplicity of the riverside; from listening to the Jewish Scriptures to making a commitment to Jesus; from mixing dyes for aristocrats to: carrying water for the baptism of a jailer; offering hospitality to missionaries; sharing her home with women who were abused and used as sources of financial gain for the greedy; breaking bread with the poor; and evangelising the spiritually impoverished. We pray that following her example, we may pause as we approach each bend in our river of life, reflect in your presence, and only move forward when, in the stillness of your peace we feel that with Lydia we are worthy to say to you and to your people: *"If you have judged me to be faithful, come to my house and stay."* Amen.

NOTES

1 Edited by Raymond E. Brown, SS., Joseph A. Fitzmyer, SJ., & Roland E. Murphy, O.Cam. *The New Jerome Biblical Commentary*. Prentice Hall, Englewood Cliffs, New Jersey. 1990, 1968. p. 753.

2 Herbert Lockyer. *All the Women of the Bible*. Zondervan Publications, Grand Rapids, Michigan. 1967. p. 84.

3 Joanne Turpin. *Twelve Apostolic Women*. St Anthony Messenger Press, Cincinnati, Ohio. 2004. pp. 76-77.

4 *Catechism of the Catholic Church*. Geoffrey Chapman, London. Revised Edition 1999. No. 1655.

5 Clarice J Martin. The Acts of the Apostles in *Searching the Scriptures* Vol 2. Ed. Elizabeth Schüssler Fiorenza. Crossroads Publ., New York. 1994. p. 784.

6 Joanne Turpin. *Twelve Apostolic Women*. St Anthony Messenger Press, Cincinnati, Ohio. 2004. p. 84.

7 Ibid.

8 Gail R. O'Day. "Acts" in *Women's Bible Commentary*, Eds. Carol A. Newsom and Sharon H Ringe. Westminster John Knox Press, Louisville, Kentucky. 1998. p. 400.

9 Edited by Raymond E. Brown, SS., Joseph A Fitzmyer, SJ., & Roland E. Murphy, O.Cam. *The New Jerome Biblical Commentary*. Prentice Hall, Englewood Cliffs, New Jersey. 1990, 1968. p. 754.

10 Carolyn Custis James. *Lost Women of the Bible*. Zondervan, Michigan, 2005. p. 215. Custis James sees men and women having been designated by Paul to take equal roles in developing and nurturing the emerging church.

11 Vatican Council II, Volume 1, Dominican Publications, Dublin. New Revised Edition 1996, *Lumen Gentium*, No. 11.

Sapphira: Straying from the Spirit and Settling with Satan

Peter said to her, "Tell me whether you sold the land for so much." And she said, "Yes, for so much." But Peter said to her, "How is it that you have agreed together to tempt the Spirit of the Lord?"

Acts 5:8,9a

The story of the fall from grace of Sapphira and her husband Ananias is one of the most dramatic and tragic scenes in the Acts of the Apostles. "It offends modern sensibilities and defies any rational or psychological explanation. The harshness of the story can be neither softened nor explained away."[1] Sapphira and her husband Ananias were a Christian married couple who created the first crisis in the new faith community. Having already died spiritually they were struck dead physically because of their deception of the Holy Spirit and the apostles. Theirs is the first fall from grace in the post Pentecost church. Sapphira is the first woman to be singled out for special mention and to have her story told in theatrical style in the Jerusalem church.

She and her husband had been amongst the group who were baptised in the Holy Spirit on Pentecost Sunday. They had been a central part of the praying community and witnessed the life which the disciples had agreed to live in common without pressure or expectation. They wanted to join that community. Following the example of new members such as Barnabas who sold his property and donated the entire proceeds to the apostles (Acts 4:36-37), they sold their property with the intention of donating the proceeds to the apostles for the daily upkeep of the community and the service of the poor. Luke recounts their story as follows:

... a man named Ananias, with the consent of his wife Sapphira, sold a piece of property; with his wife's knowledge, he kept back some of the proceeds, and brought only a part and laid it at the apostles' feet. "Ananias," Peter asked, "why has Satan filled your heart to lie to the Holy Spirit and to keep back part of the proceeds of the land? While it remained unsold, did it not remain your own? And after it was sold, were not the proceeds at your disposal? How is it that you have contrived this deed in your heart? You did not lie to us but to God!" Now when Ananias heard these words, He fell down and died. And great fear seized all those who heard of it. The young men came and wrapped up his body, then carried him out and buried him.

After an interval of about three hours his wife came in, not knowing what had happened. Peter said to her, "Tell me whether you and your husband sold the land for such and such a price." And she said, "Yes, that was the price." Then Peter said to her, "How is it that you have agreed together to tempt the Spirit of the Lord? Look the feet of those who have buried your husband are at the door, and they will carry you out." Immediately she fell down at his feet and died. When the young men

*came in they found her dead, so they carried her
out and buried her beside her husband.*

Acts 5:1-10

It was the earnest desire of Sapphira and her husband
to make a key contribution to the proclaiming and
witnessing community. They were filled with an
excitement similar to that felt by the discipleship on
Pentecost and enthusiastic for mission; but possibly
lacking the in-depth catechetical foundation necessary
for those who felt called to make an unconditional
commitment in the Spirit. Like all the other members
of the community they were fragile human beings,
worked from clay by the Creator and intended for
greatness in the Kingdom. But in their new found
enthusiasm they forgot their human frailty and need
for that Divine guidance which is the fruit of
consistent prayer.[2]

Satan was quick to notice little flaws appearing.
He edged his way gently and silently into his new
home when the couple were at their most vulnerable
having just sold their home. He led Ananias to
distrust the Mediterranean concept of reciprocal
solidarity, protection and common sustenance within
the group as observed by the new community. Unsure
of the thoughts going through his mind, Ananias
placed his reservations before his wife with the
proposal that they keep back some of the money as
security. Equally flawed, and feeling the need for
a level of independence and control, she willingly
agreed with him to engage in impression management. While culpability was clearly shared equally,
and Ananias was the first of the pair to suffer an
untimely death coupled with exclusion from God

and the faith community, this study will concentrate on Sapphira's role in the first sin of the first couple in the new Spirit-centred church.

We need look no further than the Creation Myth in the book of Genesis to find a parallel in the first created couple (Gen 3:1-24). Satan encouraged Eve to seek control, independence and equality with God. The pattern in the two stories is remarkably similar: The appearance of Satan; the flawed woman reflecting on her situation; her need for independence and control; the hiding and lying to God in spiritual death; and the exclusion of the couple from God's presence. Lying was central to the original fall from grace in Genesis. It was also prominent in the original sin of the original couple in the New Testament. Central to both stories stands the woman who in both cases has a position of power over her husband. Adam would not have eaten the apple had Eve not encouraged him to do so. Ananias would not have tried to cheat the Holy Spirit if Sapphira had not given him her unconditional support.

Whether the couple are "historical people who actually died suddenly or whether they are a symbol of death is not really relevant. For Luke the truth is that, regardless of the many pitfalls and threats, persecution, trials, and failures, the Gospel is spread through the power of the Holy Spirit residing in the Church."[3] Those who fail to collaborate with the Holy Spirit falter in their own spiritual and prayer life, and so, die to the Spirit. In so doing, they exclude themselves from the mission of furthering the reign of God because they create new priorities for themselves. Sapphira's original sin, related to the use of property, something that has had a powerful hold on humanity from the moment when God entrusted the entire earth to the original couple in Eden (Gen 2:15).

Property and the use of money were central concerns for Luke throughout his Gospel. He raises them as forceful teaching points for Jesus in at least thirteen of the twenty-four chapters in his Gospel. Their abuse, misuse and misappropriation are areas of concern for God throughout Old Testament times too, as is illustrated by the stories of men such as Achan (Josh 7:1-26) and Saul (1 Sam 15:1-35). Both men, in their own time: Achan during the fall of Jericho about 1234 BC, as a leading member of the successful army, and Saul as King in about the year 1018 BC, led Israel to victory. However, each in turn allowed himself to be tempted by Satan and disobeyed God's command to leave the battle site without taking any of the enemy's property.

Achan took a fine robe from Shinar, two hundred shekels of silver and an ingot of gold weighing fifty shekels. Despite his acknowledgement of his sin and plea for forgiveness on being challenged by Joshua, the people stoned him to death. They recognised that he had already died to the Holy Spirit's voice.

Saul in his turn was rejected as king by God for having disobeyed Samuel's command to destroy everything belonging to the Amalekites once his army had conquered them in battle. However, Saul yielded to the temptation of Satan to hold on to all the best of the cattle, fatlings, sheep, lambs and all that was valuable belonging to the defeated Amalekites. When challenged by Samuel who, like Peter in the story of Sapphira, was divinely inspired to raise questions, Saul admitted his guilt but insisted that he had withheld the stock so that his people could sacrifice them to God. Samuel advised him that God is not so much honoured by burned offerings as by obedience and integrity (15:22-23). Like his predecessor Achan, Saul had died to the Spirit before ever God excluded him in physical death from his position amongst God's people.

Luke would have been familiar with this history and keen to alert the new community to the dangers of riches, and the need for constant vigilance and prayer. They too, would probably recall the fate of the original couple and of some of those whose great potential for service and holiness in the Israel of the Old Covenant was destroyed by their greed and bad behaviour. Luke's objective was to make clear that when individual members of the community fail in truth, charity, generosity, or service the whole community is weakened. Furthermore, the witness value of the church is called into question, and its potential to attract new members is decreased.

The instruction of Jesus was to proclaim the Good News to all nations beginning in Jerusalem (Lk 24:46-47), and to baptise the people in the name of the Trinity (Mt 28:19). A church damaged by the deception of its members was in no position to carry out this command. It was, therefore, the will of God, as in Old Testament times that fatally flawed members should be debarred from the proclaiming community. Hence Sapphira who had already undergone a spiritual death, died physically to the community as well.

God, who never gives up on a sinner, had inspired Peter to question Sapphira about the money in an effort to give her the opportunity to repent. However, she rejected the offer and unlike her husband who did not answer Peter's question, she confirmed the original story. In so doing, she demonstrated that this was not a 'one off' human slip but a premeditated and determined attempt at duplicity. She was trying to deceive the Holy Spirit and Peter who was now the mouthpiece of the Holy Spirit. She had forgotten that the motivating power behind the new community was the Holy Spirit (Jn 16:7-11), and that any attempt to deceive the church was a sin against the Promise made by Jesus and welcomed by the apostles (Acts 2:4). By her own false words Sapphira called down the judgment of God on herself. She was guilty of deliberate fraud and dishonesty.

Up to this point in Acts, Luke has painted a picture of a community living in wonderful harmony. The Holy Spirit was the power engine behind this tranquil community. There was no indication of conflict, power struggle or status craving. On the surface Sapphira was part of that harmony, generosity and other worldly value system. Metaphorically speaking the Garden of Eden had been replicated. But Satan, who had failed in his efforts to tempt Jesus to seek power and control during his retreat in the desert (Mt 4:10); and to withdraw from his final redemptive act in the Garden of Gethsemane (Mk 14:35), was continuing his campaign. He had succeeded in getting Judas to succumb to the temptation to acquire a little additional finance for the community by betraying Jesus (Mt 26:15).

Furthermore, he had partially succeed in undermining Peter's faith in the courtyard of the High Priest (Lk 22:56-62). Luckily for Peter, Jesus came to the rescue, *"The Lord turned and looked at Peter.*

And Peter remembered the word of the Lord, how he had said to him, 'Before the cock crows today, you will deny me three times.' And he went out and wept bitterly." (Mt 26:74-75). Peter knew what it was to sin and to need an opportunity to repent. He renewed his commitment and his faith in a baptism of his own tears. Jesus forgave him through his compassionate gaze while at the same time anointing him with the warm chrism of mercy.

Having failed to destroy the new community through the male line alone, Satan directed his gaze once more at the female line. He had triumphed in Eden. He might well succeed again. In his new bid, he would focus once more on a woman. In Jewish society the woman was the heart in the home. Satan saw Sapphira as the aorta of the church. If he could alienate and introduce deception there, he would surely bring the church down. Sapphira was "an intellectually engaged" woman.[4] But despite this she was an easier target than Eve.

However, having received mercy himself, Peter was keen to provide the same opportunity for Sapphira. He therefore questioned her. Sadly, Satan had a firm grip and instead of confessing she persisted with her impression management. Perhaps by this stage she had begun to believe her own lies. Satan appeared to have achieved his goal. But as C.S. Lewis points out in his book *The Problem of Pain*, "the sinner is a horror to God …a creature ill-adapted to the universe… by the abuse of free will"[5]. As a surgeon removes detrimental cancer cells from the body the unrepentant sinner is removed from the discipleship. And as Jesus had defeated Satan by rising from the dead, the Holy Spirit now defeated him by excluding Sapphira from the new faith community.

No permanent damage had been done to the community. Once they regained their composure:

> *More than ever believers were added to the Lord, multitudes both of men and women, so that they even carried out the sick into the streets, and laid them on beds and pallets, that as Peter came by at least his shadow might fall on some of them. The people also gathered from the towns around Jerusalem, bringing the sick and those afflicted with unclean spirits, and they were all healed.*
>
> Acts 5:14-16

Conscious of the potential evils caused by the abuse and misuse of money, and the many teachings of Jesus on the subject and on true discipleship: The Beatitudes (Lk 6:20); the mission of the seventy-two (10:1-10); against hording possessions (12:13-15); renouncing possessions (14:28-33); the right use of money (16:9-13); tribute to Caesar (20:20-26); and the widow's mite (21:1-4), to list but a few, Luke made sure that all new members realised that the original sin in the church related to the misappropriation of money. In so doing he was giving an eschatological dimension to the property of believers. Additionally he was emphasising the importance of sharing possession in common and so eliminating the burden of poverty on the new people of God (Deut 15:3-4).

REFLECTION

There are many similarities between the Old Testament myth concerning Eve and the New Testament story of Sapphira. Both women had husbands who trusted them. Each was mistress of her household and had control over her husband. Eve hid in the garden when God appeared. Sapphira hid the truth about the money when Peter provided her with an opportunity to tell the truth and to repent.

Bearing in mind that in the Old Testament, Achan and Saul were equally easily tempted by Satan, we must be careful not to think that it is only women who are easily deceived. Neither must we think that women are more attracted by power and a need to control than men.

We need to be aware too, that in each case the woman had a male partner who could have acted with integrity. The challenge is to reflect on the human condition. No member of the human family is above deceit. It is only the power of the Holy Spirit working in the community that prevents humanity from self destruction. It is prayer alone that keeps the creature in tune with the Creator. The reflective reading of Sacred Scripture keeps us alert to our privileges and our responsibilities as children of the New Covenant. It also encourages us to be watchful to the needs of our neighbour, the right use of money, property and the natural resources of the earth. Sapphira's fall from grace was probably a gradual one. Being conscientious, abstemious, faithful, straight forward and honest in the smallest areas of the Christian life; and in the use of the earth's resources is an insurance policy against great disasters for ourselves and our successors.

- Why has Luke placed the story of Sapphira and her husband so early in his story of the Post Pentecost church?

- Nowadays we are constantly reminded to work positively to prevent any increase in global warming and to make every possible effort to avoid it. Are there easy and simple ways in which we could exercise economy in our use of natural resources in our own homes?

- Might it ease our worries about leaving our carbon footprint behind us if we chose to walk to the shops, church and the garden centre rather than driving our cars?

In our affluent, technologically-driven and sophisti-cated yet, frequently empty society today, we need to learn anew that nothing that has been created is for our use alone. Everything we receive, earn through honest work, or inherit from other lawful sources is a gift from God. It is given out of love and intended to be used in making a positive contribution to the on-going work of creation in which we are partners with the Creator. That partnership calls on women and men alike, to become selfless team mates in witnessing to the reign of God in the world and to be active and unconditional collaborators in pro-claiming the Good News.

The discipleship of equals, who lived life in common and donated all their proceeds to the upkeep of the community and the betterment of the poor, lonely, vulnerable and the mentally and physically ill continues to work in our Church today. They greet all nations in the form of those who work for SCIAF,

Trocaire, CAFOD and Mary's Meals, to name but a few international Catholic Charities. They are active here in these islands through the Society of St Vincent de Paul, the Sisters of Mercy and the Missionaries of Charity who never let a needy person pass their doors without offering sustenance, compassion and care. They bring life to the most vulnerable members of our communities in places such as the Wayside in Glasgow which provides a warm welcome, a comfortable place to relax and converse, good food and warm clothes on a three hundred and sixty-five days a year basis; the many homes run by the Jericho Benedictine Brothers who provide accommodation and care so lovingly for those who suffer from so many different forms of addiction, rehabilitate them, prepare them for useful employment and keep a watchful eye out for them as they struggle to keep a job and remain 'clean' and 'dry'.

- How honest are we in relation to the use of resources which are provided for our use in our place of work? Do we sometimes 'borrow' or use them to facilitate our own and our families needs?

- How genuinely generous are we towards the mission, the poor, immigrants and asylum seekers to our area?

- What provision does our church make for the most vulnerable in our society e.g. those addicted to drugs, alcohol and gambling?

- Does our Diocese, as opposed to our Religious Congregations, make provision for our suffering and broken brothers and sisters?

Conscious of the old proverb: "Give me a fish and I'll eat for a day; teach me to fish and I'll eat for a life-time", we might be enriched by re-considering how the money we raise through agencies such as CAFOD, SCIAF and Trocaire is spent. We need to consider whether or not it is spent directly on the desperate foundational needs of our starving and destitute brothers and sisters in the third world. We might be enriched by asking ourselves if more could be done in terms of providing wells, basic housing, irrigation systems, better quality education and transport structures instead of funding 'affirmation visits' from overseas.

- How much of the money donated to our Catholic and Christian Charities is spent on 'red carpet' visits of 'ambassadors', their entourages and paid staff, as opposed to making provision that will ensure long term structural contributions to the life of the poor?

- What provision is made for our dedicated volunteers who cannot offer money but who give generously of their invaluable skills?

- How ethical are some of the ways in which donations are sought for campaign funding by those who desire to become public representatives?

- What about the methods engaged in by our so called Christian politicians and their supporters when both raising and using acquired funds?

- In our social and business relations do we make truth and honesty our priorities; or do we try to be politically correct on all occasions telling ourselves that we are being protective of the feelings of others when in reality it is our own status, career prospects or other private interests we are shielding?

Sapphira, like her husband had been baptised in the Holy Spirit. As intelligent adults, they had gone down into the tomb with Jesus and been raised up to live as Kingdom people. Initially their hearts were full of joy and they joined the new community with an unconditional commitment to witness and proclamation. Sadly they became diverted and in a short space of time they began to slip from the Spirit to Satan, from the eagle to the evil one. That which is transient gripped them with a control that became fixed. Possibly without realising it, they lost their vision of God, of wholeness and of the authentic. Once they arrived on Mount Compromise, they gradually slid into the clutches of Satan leaving the Eagle hovering in another space. Sapphira was her husband's confidant. Had she continued to journey with the Spirit, she would, as mistress of the household, have been in a position to get her husband to reflect further on his proposition in the light of his Christian faith and to have rejected Satan and taken refuge in the Spirit.

It is still true that in most societies today women continue to hold a special place at the heart of the home. While Luke makes very clear that both genders are meant to learn from this story, it speaks in a special way to women. They, because of the birthing process through which they go in giving life to their children, have a unique relationship with them, and a special duty to be positive role models and witness to the Good News. Just as Mary made a home for Jesus within her young and fragile body, women continue to form the womb of the church today. They have a distinctive duty to transmit the faith to their children and to teach them to pray. They also have a profound duty, in partnership with their husbands, to bring their children up aware of their privilege as members of the New Covenant Community who know how to journey with the Spirit in integrity, and to fly with the Eagle in mercy and love.

As part of our meditation on the story of Sapphira, we might be further enriched by considering some of the following questions:

- Are we really aware of how sinful it is to engage in impression management, and the dangers to which such behaviour exposes us?

- In our current self-centred and ambitious society is there anything we can do to help people to see that material possessions are transitory and that it is only in working to bring glory to God that real happiness is found?

- If God chose to make a physical visit to our community during Sunday Liturgy, or to our home during Sunday lunch what might be the judgment that would be made on our integrity, single mindedness, generosity and our conversations?

Let us pray

Provident God, I come before you as a penitent pleading for pardon and peace.

I regret the times when I have had the audacity to tell you that I desired to make your Kingdom a living reality, while I ignored the pain, poverty and homelessness of my brothers and sisters.

I am sorry that I was selfish enough to pray to you for my own daily bread while I ignored the needs of others; gave only from my surplus to the poor, and forgot to reach out to missionaries.

As I confess my sinfulness, I ask myself what right have I to ask you to protect me from evil when I use and abuse the resources of this earth in terms of electricity, oil, fuel, wood, paper and synthetic materials as though there was no need to think about tomorrow; when I never lift a hand to help or greet with a smile, the person who lives next door to me; when I am too lazy to make a visit to a hospital patient or a prisoner who has no one to care for them.

Merciful God, forgive me for deluding myself and thinking that I am better than Sapphira.

I resolve now to renew and to live my baptismal promises and to be faithful to my prayer life, to use the earth's resources sparingly; to reach out to others generously and to journey with the Holy Spirit confident of your love and mercy. Amen.

NOTES

1   Gail R. O'Day. "Acts" in *Women's Bible Commentary*, Eds. Carol A. Newsom and Sharon H. Ringe. Westminster John Knox Press, Louisville, Kentucky. 1998. p. 398.

2   Sue & Larry Richards. *Every Woman in the Bible*. Nelson Publishers, Nashville. 1999. p. 236.

3   Mary Anne Getty-Sullivan. *Women in the New Testament*. The Liturgical Press, Collegeville, Minnesota. 2001. p. 146.

4   Clarice J. Martin, The Acts of the Apostles in *Searching the Scriptures* Vol 2. Ed. Elizabeth Schüssler Fiorenza. Crossroads Publ., New York. 1994. p. 780.

5   C.S. Lewis. *The Problem of Pain*. Fount Paperbacks Collins, London. 1986. p.55.

Euodia and Syntyche:
Faith, Friendship, Fragility and Fidelity

*I entreat Eu-o'dia and I entreat Syn'tyche to agree
in the Lord. And I ask you also, true yokefellow,
help these women, for they have laboured side by
side with me in the gospel together with Clement
and the rest of my fellow workers, whose names
are in the book of life.* Phil 4:2-3

Euodia and Syntyche were two Christian women who
had come to the fullness of faith through Paul's
mission in Philippi, during his second missionary
journey. They were inhabitants of a multicultural
and multifaith city where cults flourished. The city's
customs and practices differed sharply from those of
other centres in the Roman Empire. Women and
men stood on an equal footing in every area of life,
work and worship. In contrast with Jewish and
Roman practice, women frequently took leadership
positions in religious ritual, prayer and worship.

Their influence in the community of Philippi was
far greater than that of women in either Jerusalem
or Rome. Conscious of this and how easily groups
and cults can become fractured and fragmented, Paul
made it his pastoral priority to guide and protect the
unity and single mindedness of his infant church.
He had been alerted to the fact that what may have
started as a private, dispute between Euodia and
Syntyche, had taken a grip on the wider community

and begun to divide it. He was determined to help in restoring positive relationships as discreetly and respectfully as possible. Hence his heartfelt plea to the community in general, and in particular to the two women who were his friends in leadership.

Do nothing from selfishness or conceit, but in humility count others better than yourselves. Let each of you look not only to his own interests, but also to the interests of others. Have this mind among yourselves, which is yours in Christ Jesus, who, though he was in the form of God, did not count equality with God a thing to be grasped, but emptied himself, taking the form of a servant, being born in the likeness of [humankind]. Phil 2:3-7

On arrival in the city, in about 50 AD, his first converts had been women. Together with his companions Silas and Luke, he established a warm, friendly and respectful relationship with them, making Lydia's home the area's first house church (Acts 16:15). This easy pastoral relationship would be characteristic of all his associations with the area. Although he had not been in the Upper Room on Pentecost Sunday, he worked in a spirit that reflected its warmth and friendship. In his letter, it is not surprising that he sends greetings to *"all the saints in Christ Jesus who are at Philip'pi"* (Phil 1:1). Despite its cultural and ethnic diversity, each member of this community was precious to Paul, in true Jewish and early Christian fashion he referred to them as 'saints' (2 Chr 6:41; Ps 16:3; Prov 2:8; Dan 8:24; Acts 26:10). In his view 'the communion of saints' was already a reality.

The Philippians had welcomed the Good News and were, therefore, amongst God's most holy and select peoples. His two-fold desire for them, once they had been baptised, was that they would continue to avail themselves of the evangelisation provided and see their conversion as an on-going process until they became totally immersed in Jesus Christ, *"who, though he was in the form of God, did not count equality with God a thing to be grasped, but emptied himself, taking the form of a servant"* (Phil 2:6-7). Paul had found the Philippian women in particular hungry for the Gospel, for its family and moral values; and for its message of healing, peace and salvation through Jesus Christ.

Despite much that has been written about his lack of appreciation of women and his seeming failure to establish life-giving relationships with them in Jewish circles, Paul seems to have inculturated both himself and his message with ease in Philippi. He was actually the first member of the Council of Jerusalem to accept women as leaders in what had, apparently been until then, a male dominated executive. *"…they have laboured side by side with me in the gospel together with Clement and the rest of my fellow workers, whose names are in the book of life"* (4:3b). In our time many women and men wonder how the Church, not only in Europe, but globally, has managed to forget the importance of genuine in-depth inculturation at leadership and other levels.

This letter from Paul to his foundational European community is generally viewed as one of his most pastoral and affirming of women in the ministry of leadership. While biblical researchers see it as a blending of at least three letters, written with great joy, heartfelt concern for community unity (1:27; 2:25; 3:13-4; 4:2-3) and, in a special way, in the great hymn calling for total surrender to Jesus Christ (2:6-11); anxiety about misrepresentation of the truth (3:1b-4:1), gratitude and affection (4:10-20); we have received it as a unit in the New Testament.

Although its overall content relates to the unity of the church in general, it has a special message for the relationship and ministry of Euodia and Syntyche: reconciliation is essential if their ministry is to be truly redemptive (4:2). Despite the fact that Paul had to leave the community following his initial ninety day stay with Lydia (Acts 16:15b, 40), their concerns were his too. He knew the value of this community and particularly that of these two fine but flawed women. As a responsible leader, he was not going to allow human frailty to destroy the unity of his first European foundation. He had been careful to provide pastoral care, theological input and spiritual direction for the community either through quick visits (Acts 20:1-2,6), or through his loyal co-worker Timothy. He would not let them down when thunder rumbled in their skies:

> *I hope in the Lord Jesus to send Timothy to you soon, so that I may be cheered by news of you. I have no one like him, who will be genuinely anxious for your welfare. They all look after their own interests, not those of Jesus Christ.*
>
> *But Timothy's worth you know, how as a son with a father he has served with me in the gospel. I hope therefore to send him just as soon as I see how it will go with me.* Phil 2:19-22

Paul makes clear that as he writes, he is in prison (1:18), and that he is suffering for the sake of the Gospel. He goes on to emphasise that just as he suffers for Jesus, his favourite community must expect to suffer too. Here he was acknowledging not only the persecution which faced the Philippian community, but also the internal suffering because of the disunity. In fact much of the letter "revolves around the idea of *koinónia*, 'common participation': *koinónia* in suffering intensifies the union between apostle and community".[1] Paul's physical suffering is clearly added to by his anxiety over the community, and especially by the on-going rift between Euodia and Syntyche. His hope is that if they can be given time, space and gentle encouragement, they will, as a gesture to him, and in empathy with his suffering, resolve their differences.

Considerable work remains to be done on this letter in terms of gynocentric interpretations for three reasons: the need to seek objectivity in relation to the place and value of women's ministry in Scripture; to fully understand their true place in the context of the mother church in Europe; and to enable a male-led Church in particular and women in general to learn credible lessons about the authentic rights and natural abilities of women for leadership in the Church today.[2] It is not often mentioned that Junia went to prison for the Gospel (Rom 17:7); and that as early as the second century women such as Perpetua and Felicity were commemorated as martyrs for the faith.[3]

Many scholars believe that while writing this letter, Paul was serving his sentence in Ephesus, while some argue that he was in Rome. This latter is unlikely as

Rome was 800 miles away by sea or more than a month's journey. Ephesus, on the other hand was only a week to ten days journey from Philippi. In his letter Paul states as his hope, *"that shortly I myself shall come"* to Philippi (2:24). In the light of this, it is generally accepted that the letter was written from prison in Ephesus, sometime between 54 and 58 AD.[4] There Paul was actually within easy reach of Philippi and could have the letter delivered to the community by either Timothy who was one of his most loyal companions, or possibly their own Epaphroditus whom they, the church community of Philippe, had sent with financial aid and as a pastoral support to Paul:

> *I have thought it necessary to send to you Epaphrodi'tus my brother and fellow worker and fellow soldier, and your messenger and minister to my need, for he has been longing for you all, and has been distressed because you heard that he was ill.*   Phil 2:25-26

By 55-58 AD Paul was an experienced missionary and leader who had learned that apportioning blame in situations where clarity is possibly clouded, only serves to anger, alienate and enlarge division. He knew the value of situational as well as servant leadership and he was not going to appear to adopt a prophetic approach until he had explored every possible dimension of the unique circumstances in which the two women found themselves. Keeping them in mind, and using the self emptying Jesus as a model he pleaded with the community as whole one more time:

Let each of you look not only to his [her] own interests, but also to the interests of others. Have this mind among yourselves, which is yours in Christ Jesus, who, though he was in the form of God, did not count equality with God a thing to be grasped, but emptied himself, taking the form of a servant, being born in the likeness of men. And being found in human form he humbled himself and became obedient unto death, even death on a cross.

Phil 2:4-8

Some scholars suggest that as Epaphroditus was returning to Philippi, Paul may have chosen to use him as his '*yokefellow*', or facilitator to help bring the Euodia and Syntyche disagreement to a conclusion after they had failed to appropriate to themselves, his more general advice on unity to the community as a whole. Epaphroditus later became the first bishop of Philippi and was known to the Romans as Erastus. He is now honoured as a saint in both the Greek Orthodox and the Greek Catholic Churches. Paul speaks of Euodia and Syntyche as women who *have "laboured side by side with me in the gospel"* (4:3b). Scholars believe that this means that they took the missionary work seriously and devoted their lives to it as leaders and may even have been on other missions with Paul.

Although he says that their names are written in the book of life thus paying them the highest possible honour; it is clear from the overall content of his letter that a share in the Beatific Vision is not an automatic right. The struggle to transcend self and embrace the cross, in whatever form it presents itself, are the criteria by which names gain a permanent place in the book of life. Citizenship of heaven was prized by those Romans who accepted baptism, above their imperial heritage. Those who accepted baptism from outside of Rome such as Euodia and Syntyche welcomed it as a privilege and a grace. However, like all privileges it carried responsibilities. Central to these were the virtues of fidelity, love, forgiveness and reconciliation. None could be more aware of this than the two women who laboured side by side with Paul for the Gospel.

Disagreements in male-male, male-female and female-female relationships are not unknown in sacred scripture. Martha and Mary had their differences about hospitality (Lk 10:38-42), the mother of the sons of Zebedee caused conflict amongst the twelve when she asked Jesus for special places in the kingdom for her boys (Mt 20:20-28), Paul and Barnabas parted company for a long time over Mark (Acts 15:37-40). The disagreement between Euodia and Syntyche has tended to be written off by androcentric interpreters of this letter as almost insignificant. This is surely a misrepresentation of the situation. It demonstrates that this is one of the areas of scripture that awaits further in-depth social analysis and detailed theological critiquing by women scholars in the future. The upset caused Paul immense concern and had the potential to tear the community apart. While, in the light of current scholarship, it does not appear to have related to either doctrinal or theological matters, it had the potential to destroy the infant church in Europe.

It was absolutely essential, for example that when the community met for its weekly prayer, worship and Eucharist, there was an atmosphere of unity, love and sharing. If there were factions operating, and clearly there were, this would make a mockery of the celebration: *"So if you are offering your gift at the altar, and there remember that your brother has something against you, leave your gift there before the altar and go; first be reconciled to your brother [or sister], and then come and offer your gift"* (Mt 5:23-24). Reconciliation was a pre-requisite for worship and celebration. Paul had already shown himself to be conscious of this in his first letter to the Corinthian community (1 Cor 11:17-27). The celebration had to be presided over by a recognised leader. It is possible that if it was held in a household headed by a presiding male the division might not be obvious. In this case of the two women it was a painful wound and it had to be healed for the sake of the Gospel.

It is for this reason the Paul felt obliged to address it in a public letter. While he made his concern known to the entire community, he was careful to craft his appeal in pastoral language and to '*entreat*', as opposed to command or direct. His is a totally non-judgmental approach. He does not threaten with excommunication or suspension; nor does he ensure that they are directly or indirectly excluded from ministry. His approach is that of Jesus (Jn 8:7). His is a plea from the heart. His desire is to reconcile and make whole again as opposed to divide, demean or diminish. Both his attitude and his style are very different from those which he took with the Corinthians' conflict (1 Cor 1:10-20). In his plea he does not ask that they apply the principles of diplomacy or social justice but the mind, '*phronein*' of Jesus Christ who, as he had so often reminded them: *"though he was in the form of God, did not count equality with God a thing to be grasped, but emptied himself, taking the form of a servant, being born in the likeness of men. And being found in human form he humbled himself and became obedient unto death, even death on a cross"* (Phil 2:6b-8).

The Greek word *'phronein'* meaning same mind or mutual understanding, appears eight times in the short letter. It indicates clearly that Paul sought collaboration and a united Christian partnership above all else. It is possible that in light of the damage already done to the community neither woman deserved this heart-centred caring, but each received it as a free gift. His pastoring did not end with an even-handed approach and compassionate words. He went the extra mile (Mt 8:38-48), by sending a facilitator whose name, as mentioned above, is not recorded. Mary Getty Sullivan comments that it is strange that Paul does not mention Lydia (Acts 16:14, 40), whom Luke later identifies as the founding patron of the Philippian community.[5] She goes on to propose that indeed Lydia could have been the real *'yokefellow'*.

Scripture does not tell us if the two women resolved their differences but we can be sure that they did because Paul never refers to it again and we know that Epaphroditus later became bishop of Philippi. Polycarp, writing about the Philippians in the second century commented in a letter that they "have followed the example of true love and have helped on their way, as opportunity offered, those who were bound in chains." This is surely proof that Paul's mission was successfully accomplished. He left Philippi the legacy of a united and mission-minded community whose leaders had graduated to maturity in Christ Jesus.

An issue clearly arose between two great and saintly women who once shared a wonderful friendship. It is obvious from the over-all content of Paul's letter to the Philippians that he was keenly aware of the damage that any misunderstanding or cooling in a friendship at leadership level could do to an entire group or community. Euodia and Syntyche were clearly intelligent, educated and economically secure women whose love for truth and commitment to the moral and ethical values of the Gospel led them to Christ and to membership of the church co-founded by Lydia and Paul. Having accepted the role of leaders whether as deaconesses, 'faith friends' or leaders of house churches, they had a high degree of influence in the local and wider community. With this went a great level of responsibility of which they would have been very well aware.

However it is possible that in their enthusiasm for the Gospel and in their efforts to bring as many people as possible to Jesus their vision became blurred, and they engaged in some form of competition or isolationism. Whatever their differences and however praiseworthy or self-righteous each may have assessed her intention to be, Paul was troubled enough to feel it necessary to intervene in an effort to being some enlightenment to the situation and to help them to revisit their baptismal commitment.

Contrary to Roman and Jewish theories and practices in resolving disputes Paul concentrates on gospel values as laid down by Jesus in his Sermon on the Mount (Mt 5:23-24). He makes clear that human and worldly judgments have no place in the reign of

God. He calls for compassion, mutual understanding, forgiveness and mercy. The concept of justice does not even feature in his discernment. His is to be a community that is nurtured not on legalism but on the Spirit and on the virtue of mercy.

Paul appointed a '*yokefellow*', a facilitator to ensure that the dispute was brought to a happy conclusion. The term yoke is generally viewed as negative in Christian thinking because of the cross (Mt 11:29-30). However, in the agricultural area of the middle, near East and Europe of the time, a yoke would be seen as a wonderfully supportive device. It was a piece of wood that was used as a type of crossbar which held two animals together in a working situation, thus ensuring that the burden being pulled, as in a plough, or being drawn as in a cart, was shared equally between the two animals. So Paul intended his facilitator to become an equal partner with the women in processing their pain in a way that would end in harmony and mutual appreciation.

Much of this particular letter centres on the idea of suffering in *koinonia*, "common participation": a suffering which intensifies the union between apostle and community. While suffering an unjust imprisonment Paul was forced into physical as well as mental suffering. This is added to by news of the on-going discord in his favourite community, and especially by that of the rift between Euodia and Syntyche.

- How might these two wonderful but flawed women be helped by reflecting on how the disciples worked together following the descent of the Holy Spirit on Pentecost Sunday?

- Do you see your conversion as an on-going process? If you do, how do you insure that you are journeying in the right direction?

- How might we who are free show that we: (a) Suffer with our brothers and sisters in communist countries today and: (b) How might we ensure that our shared suffering is fruitful?

- What might cause such a rift in your local church today?

Although Luke does not say that the problem was resolved, Polycarp makes very clear that it certainly was, and that the community not only faced persecution for the faith, cheerfully and defiantly but that they reached out in support of their suffering sisters and brothers in other areas. It was Paul's desire that ideas about human honours, social status, rights and ranks should never be a source of motivation in the faith community. To him it was a spiritual concept and relationship and its central focus should always be Jesus, the suffering servant who humbled himself so that humanity might be liberated and restored to its original relationship with its Creator.

Paul was not speaking to slaves and the marginalised in this letter. He was concerned with spiritual and social leaders, business people, government officials, financiers and entrepreneurs who had easy access to the written word and who were in a situation to make a difference to the community's quality of life and faith. He wanted all to see Jesus as their paradigm and to direct their focus on the reign of God as opposed to the reign of Satan or the Emperor.

Paul makes clear that while sacrifice is trans-formative in terms of grace it must come from the heart of each person and not be enforced by an external agent or agency. Pressure exerted by an external agent is an act of injustice and must be resisted. Ultimately Gospel values are only nurtured by heart-service which is the fruit of living a reflective life supported by prayer. "The liberative content of the Gospel cannot be compromised by a false acceptance of a cross that does not build justice".[6] In our third millennium church, women and the poor continue to be encouraged to see injustices such as poverty, staying within abusive relationships and being discriminated against as sharing in the cross of Jesus. They are frequently told that the patient bearing of their suffering now assures that their names are written in *"the book of life"* (Phil 4:3).

This is a falsification and a misinterpretation of the Beatitudes (Mt 5:3-11), and a misguided theology. Suffering is redemptive when accepted graciously, worked through and transcended. It is not redemptive when it is blindly accepted and the perpetrators are enabled to extend it, benefit from it or destroy their victims. As a moral theologian friend of mine once commented: "It is how you come out of it, not how you got into it, or chose to die under it that matters."

- What is your understanding of participation in the cross and the sufferings of Jesus?

- If you were asked by either your local church or by a member of the episcopate to become a yokebearer in a dispute today would you feel able to accept the invitation?

- If you did accept such an unenviable invitation what might you learn from Paul's approach?

It is God's intention that in a truly Gospel centred church and world each human person regardless of creed, colour, gender or ethnicity will in reality, live now and every day of their lives in the consciousness of their heavenly citizenship. Each human person is called upon, with Paul, to proclaim a gospel of partnership, mutual support, equality, freedom, unity and joy as the true ingredients for a life lived in the Spirit. Paul makes clear that a place at the Paschal Banquet is not an automatic right; nor is it granted on the basis of social status, blind acceptance of unjust suffering or family genes. It is earned through fidelity to the promises made at baptism, and a life lived in faith, hope and love.

- What might we learn from Paul in relation to partnership in ministry today?

- When you read about scandals or disputes in the Institutional Church today, how do you feel and react?

- In our world what do we mean when we speak of selfish ambition? Can you think of areas where either members of the government or local council representatives might be accused of selfish ambition?

- What about our local church: Are there times when conflict is generated by people whose central motivation is the promotion of self? How does such behaviour impact on the lives of the community?

- How might committed Christians who are victims of injustice, violence, family break-up, infidelity or bereavement be supported by Church leadership?

Paul follows four distinct steps in relation to conflict resolution in his communications with Euodia and Syntyche:

1. a plea that they find a way forward together in Jesus. This did not invite human judgements or a measured hand in apportioning blame. No, Paul wants a meeting of minds centred on Jesus;

2. provides a 'yokefellow' a wise and discerning person who would journey with the women and enable them to speak their truth in humility to each other, to listen with discerning ears and to embrace the truth with understanding hearts;

3. encourages them to consider the history of their relationship, coming to faith and their shared ministry;

4. pleads with them to consider their future in view of the fact that both of their names have been inscribed in the book of life. He then leaves them to work out their issues under the guidance of the Holy Spirit, while encouraging them to: *"Rejoice in the Lord always; again I will say, Rejoice"* (Phil 4:4).

It was Paul's earnest wish that not only should the two women resolve their differences but that the entire church at Philippi should re-examine itself and then re-commit itself in such a way that 'the mind of Christ' would become a characteristic of the entire community. It continues to be his prayer for both the local church, as in each parish, and the Institutional Church, as in the Magisterium in our time and in the future.

- How might we help our local community to develop the mind of Jesus Christ?

- To what degree has Church leadership both locally and globally followed Paul's example of inculturation since (a) Vatican Council II and (b) the launch of the *General Directory for Catechesis* in 1997?

- Can you think of times when internal 'church disputes' might have been better facilitated if the four steps outlined by Paul were employed?

Prayer

Provident God, we thank you for the ministry of Paul to the community at Philippi. We thank you especially that your Holy Spirit empowered him to inculturate himself compassionately and successfully into that mixed and varied community. Thank you for giving him the grace to see that women and men are called to equal partnership in the ministry of proclamation and witness.

Thank you for the human frailty of that first European community, from whom we have so much to learn. Thank you for the way they struggled together in order to be faithful to the Gospel. Thank you that they challenged one another and that through their pain, and brokenness they became more faith-filled and compassionate people. Thank you for the pastoral way in which Paul facilitated reconciliation between Euodia and Syntyche, and for the giftedness of the one who acted as 'yokebearer' in enabling them to transcend self and re-engage with Jesus Christ.

May their story inspire us on our faith journey. May it help us individually, and as a community to learn that true unity is the fruit of active engagement with Gospel principles rather than passive acceptance of social trends. May we learn too, the value of discernment over apathy, mercy over malice, love over legalism and reconciliation over rank. We make this prayer in Jesus' name. Amen.

NOTES

1   Edited by Raymond E. Brown, SS., Joseph A Fitzmyer, SJ., & Roland E. Murphy, O.Cam. *The New Jerome Biblical Commentary*. Prentice Hall, Englewood Cliffs, New Jersey. 1990, 1968. p. 792.

2   Carolyn Osiek. "Philippians" in *Searching the Scriptures* Vol 2. Ed. Elizabeth Schüssler Fiorenza. Crossroads Publ., New York. 1994. p. 246.

3   Pheme Perkins. "Philippians" in *Women's Bible Commentary*, Eds. Carol A. Newsom and Sharon H Ringe. Westminster John Knox Press, Louisville, Kentucky. 1998. p. 237.

4   Edited by Raymond E. Brown, SS., Joseph A Fitzmyer, SJ., & Roland E. Murphy, O.Cam. *The New Jerome Biblical Commentary*. Prentice Hall, Englewood Cliffs, New Jersey. 1990, 1968. p. 792.

5   Mary Anne Getty-Sullivan. *Women in the New Testament*. The Liturgical Press, Collegeville, Minnesota. 2001. p. 251.

6   Carolyn Osiek. "Philippians" in *Searching the Scriptures* Vol 2. Ed. Elizabeth Schüssler Fiorenza. Crossroads Publ., New York. 1994. p. 246.

Lois and Eunice:
Grandmother, Mother and Mentor

I thank God whom I serve with a clear conscience,
as did my fathers, when I remember you constantly
in my prayers. As I remember your tears, I long
night and day to see you, that I may be filled with
joy. I am reminded of your sincere faith, a faith
that dwelt first in your grandmother Lo'is and your
mother Eunice and now, I am sure, dwells in you.

2 Tim 1:3-5

Lois and Eunice were the grandmother and mother of Timothy who became one of Paul's most faithful companions and emissaries in the evangelising mission of the early church. Scholars believe that Paul baptised Lois and Eunice in Lystra, during his first missionary journey in about 47 AD. It is most likely that when Lois came to faith in Jesus, she arranged to have Eunice and Timothy and the whole household baptised in keeping with the tradition that each household took its lead in faith from the head of the family (Acts 10:3; 16:15,31,34, 18:8; 1 Cor 1:16; 2 Tim 4:19). Eunice being a widow and a lone parent would automatically take the lead from her mother, who as the elder member and inheritor of property had responsibility for the family and all those who shared life with them. Both women who had been blest with the gift of creativity in motherhood would have been conscious of their duty to use this gift in promoting God's reign in the world.

During Paul's first visit to Lystra, the Gentile community welcomed him enthusiastically. Some of them would have heard about the descent of the Holy Spirit on Pentecost Sunday and Peter's confirmation that Jesus was indeed the fulfilment of the Promise made to Abraham. Others would have heard about Paul's conversion and ministry, from travellers and traders, before he arrived. They listened enthusiastically and many were baptised.

Their faith was increased when Paul worked his first recorded miracle in the area, by curing a man who had been crippled from birth. Paul's fame spread so widely amongst the Greco-Jewish and Gentile communities that despite traditional Jewish persecution, the town quickly became a Christian stronghold (Acts 14:8-20). Paul established a firm relationship with Lois and Eunice, amongst other women of the town, and visited them and the rest of the group whenever he returned to Lystra. So enthusiastic did the people become for the Gospel that in the early centuries of Christianity the area had its own bishop. The diocese is still a Roman Catholic titular see today.

Lystra was in the Roman Province of Galatia, now modern Turkey and still part of Asia Minor. It had been made a Roman colony in 6 BC in an effort to control the mountain tribes to the west. Shortly after the annexation a Roman road was built to link the town with Iconium which is modern day Konya. Lois, Eunice and Timothy who had lived there for many years, "represent the strongest maternal line of any family group in the New Testament."[1] The faith of the two women and their commitment to the study of their Hebrew Scripture laid a firm foundation for acceptance of the Good News of Jesus when they heard it from Paul's lips. They were so grounded in their Hebrew Scriptures that on hearing Paul speak about Jesus' life, death and resurrection, they were able to recognise Jesus as the promised Messiah and Saviour.

It was this instant and generous response to Jesus that, in the Deutero-Pauline Letter, 2 Timothy, led to the two women being paid the highest possible tribute by Paul:[2] *"I am reminded of your sincere faith, a faith that dwelt first in your grandmother Lo'is and your mother Eunice and now, I am sure, dwells in you"* (2 Tim 1:5). These words give the two women the right to stand tall beside all the other faith-filled and faithful women who are shown to have nurtured and sustained the infant church throughout the Acts of the Apostles and the Letters in the New Testament.

Both women seem to have been born of Jewish mothers and Greek fathers, and were given Greek names. They came from wealthy and aristocratic Jewish and Greek families. Their Jewish ancestors, despite having been dispersed during various conquests, particularly by the Babylonians and Persians, always returned to the land of their fathers. They longed to re-establish their religious way of life and live in the land which, they believed was God's gift to the Chosen People. Each attempted return was either obstructed or those who were successful were driven into exile yet again by colonists and persecutors. Their last great defeat was suffered at the hands of the Romans who, from in 63 BC consistently tightened their control of Judea and the surrounding region, thus forcing many of the priestly families to take their faith, customs and wealth back to parts of Asia Minor.

It was from families such as these that Lois and Eunice originated. It was women like them that having found faith, nurtured and gave hospitality to the new church. From the moment of their conversion they formed part of the backbone of the emerging church in places such as Lystra. Once Christians were banned from synagogues, these women made their homes into house churches for the Christian community. In the case of Lois, Eunice and Timothy, this arrangement was positively helpful because as an uncircumcised Jewish male he was regarded as a *mamzer* meaning bastard, and automatically excluded from the Temple and the Synagogue: *"Any uncircumcised male who is not circumcised in the flesh of his foreskin shall be cut off from his people; he has broken my covenant"* (Gen 17:14).

The Jewish Scripture actually forbade intermarriage: *"You shall not make marriages with them, giving your daughters to their sons or taking their daughters for your sons"* (Deut 7:3). However, both Lois and her daughter Eunice had married Greek men. In the Book of Genesis we also read: *"We cannot do this thing, to give our sister to one who is uncircumcised, for that would be a disgrace to us. Only on this condition will we consent to you: that you will become as we are and every male of you be circumcised"* (Gen 34:14-15). While it is possible that Lois' husband did submit to circumcision, it is most unlikely that Eunice's husband did, as he did not treasure that as a value for this son.

While religious education was seen as the duty of

the mother, circumcision was certainly the domain of the father or the rabbi. The mother's part was carried out creatively and faithfully: *"You shall therefore lay up these words of mine in your heart and in your soul; and you shall bind them as a sign upon your hand, and they shall be as frontlets between your eyes. And you shall teach them to your children, talking of them when you are sitting in your house, and when you are walking by the way, and when you lie down, and when you rise"* (Deut 11:13-19). Both Lois and Eunice knew that the foundation laid by parents and grandparents is the only one on which a child can build. They knew too, that it is the only one from which they will grow in either strength or weakness. They laid a foundation aimed at carrying Timothy through any challenge which the future could present to his faith, ethics and morals. Before passing judgement on the father's apparent failure to carry out his responsibility, it is worth remembering that in some areas of Greek society where skills in sports were highly prized, circumcision was frowned upon. Timothy's father would have been conscious of this.

All of this seems to indicate that the family were relics of the Exile and their families had become inculturated into Greek society and the Greek way of life. It is important to remember that while there was one central interpretation of Judaism, customs varied widely, from region to region; as they have always done in all religious observances and practices down through the ages.[3] Mary Getty Sullivan points out that many scholars trace the practice of matrilinear (that is, children were considered Jewish if their mother was a Jewess) Judaism back to the Exile.[4]

Such marriages would have been arranged by

parents while girls were still very young (Gen 34: 14-15). Arranged marriages frequently meant that girls as young as twelve were married to very much older men. Consequently many women found themselves widowed very early in life, and if left without an adequate inheritance, obliged to earn their living. Frequently grandmothers took responsibility for children while mothers worked. This does not seem to have been the case with either Lois or Eunice. Both of them appear to have married into their own social class and to have been left in comfortable circumstances on the death of their husbands.

And he came also to Derbe and to Lystra. A disciple was there, named Timothy, the son of a Jewish woman who was a believer; but his father was a Greek. He was well spoken of by the brethren at Lystra and Ico'nium. Paul wanted Timothy to accompany him; and he took him and circumcised him because of the Jews that were in those places, for they all knew that his father was a Greek.

Acts 16:1-3

Timothy was still only about twenty years old when Paul returned to Lystra shortly after parting company with Barnabas and following the Council of Jerusalem, in about 49 AD. So inspired was Timothy by Paul's commitment to the Gospel that he offered his services to him as a partner in mission. Like Hannah when she left Samuel in the Temple, Eunice had to relinquish her son (1 Sam 1:28). He had been a gift to her and on being called upon to give him to the proclamation of the Good News, she bowed to the Holy Spirit who had led him to the faith. God called, Timothy responded in faith. His mother and grandmother conscious of Jesus' teaching: *"No one after lighting a lamp puts it in a cellar or under a bushel, but on a stand, that those who enter may see the light"* (Lk 11:33), freed him for mission. As hosts in their house church they continued to engage creatively in promoting the Gospel and in mentoring other people in Lystra.

Eunice had nurtured him in the Scriptures and in good works. She had prepared him for mission. *"Train up a child in the way he should go, and when he is old he will not depart from it"* (Prov 22:6). Paul recognised the devotion with which Lois and Eunice had nurtured Timothy. He was old enough and experienced enough to realise that it was formation such as this that had helped Timothy to respond to the Holy Spirit and to offer his life in the proclamation of the Good News. The two women had handed on to Timothy what they had valued most in life in such an inspiring way that he felt obliged to share it with others.

Paul had Timothy circumcised not to contravene the decision taken by the apostles at the Council of Jerusalem; but to ensure that he was seen to respect the law and make him acceptable to the Jews with whom he still felt a huge need to share the Gospel.[5] In addition to this it was still expected by Jews that their fellow citizens in 'traditional Judaism', would accept, submit to, and maintain this long standing and prized Jewish practice. Paul's attitude was very much: *"To the Jews I became as a Jew, in order to win Jews; to those under the law I became as one under the law – though not being myself under the law – that I might win those under the law. To those outside the law I became as one outside the law – not being without law toward God but under the law of Christ – that I might win those outside the law"* (1 Cor 9:20-21). His focus was and always would be: salvation comes only through Jesus Christ.

Paul became a new mentor and second father to Timothy, or *Timótheos*, meaning honouring God. Maybe he was the only one he had ever known.[6] He encouraged him in the faith and taught him how to lead a mission. *"But as for you, man of God, shun all this; aim at righteousness, godliness, faith, love, steadfastness, gentleness"* (1 Tim 6:11). He addressed him as, *"my true child in the faith"* (1 Tim 1:2a). Later, in the same letter to Timothy and his Thessalonian community he wrote about the pain he felt at having to be apart from his dedicated and faithful co-worker: *"As I remember your tears, I long night and day to see you, that I may be filled with joy"* (2 Tim 1:4). Eunice and Lois had certainly established Timothy on firm ground and he valued that.

Scripture does not tell us how the Thessalonian women responded to Timothy but as Mary Ann Beavis points out, they were "undoubtedly attracted to the church by its counter cultural, liberating possibilities."[7] That Timothy was a successful missionary is clearly illustrated by Paul's praise and by the fact that Lois and Eunice had ensured that Timothy understood his obligation as the eldest, and in this case only son, to learn and transmit the faith and its traditions.[8] If these came under attack or if attempts were made to dilute them, he had a duty to defend them and to restate the principles that guided their lives. Having embraced Christianity he, in consultation with them, applied these same principles to the Gospel as he set out on his missionary work.

In the Deutero-Pauline Letters Timothy is encouraged to be faithful to the traditions and given positive examples of the service of devoted Christian women such as Lois and Eunice, his grandmother and mother (2 Tim 1:5), and of Priscilla (Prisca) and her husband Aquila (2 Tim 4:19). He is given negative examples of men in so far as men such as Hymenaeus and Alexander are recorded as, *"rejecting conscience, [and] made shipwreck of their faith"* (1 Tim 1:19-20). These were amongst a number of men who for reasons of their own turned against Paul and the Gospel. Sometimes Paul gives the impression that he was possibly not a particularly tactful and sensitive missionary when it came to relating with men who may not have felt able to meet his standards. Phygelus and Hermogenes are named as having *"turned away from me"* (2 Tim 1:15) and Hymenaeus and Philetus are discredited because they did not remain loyal but abandoned both Paul and the Good News.

In the interests of objectivity it is essential to note that Timothy is also warned, in a way that seems uncharacteristic of Paul, of the dangers posed by *"weak women, burdened with sins and swayed by various impulses, who will listen to anybody and can never arrive at a knowledge of the truth"* (2 Tim 3: 6a-7). Many scholars see references to women, such as this latter, as being post-Pauline, and demonstrating a male move in the developing church to discredit the leadership of women which had been affirmed, and greatly appreciated by Paul (Acts 16:14-15, 40; 2 Tim 1:5; 18:26; 1 Cor 1:11; Col 4:15).

In the later years of his life, Paul commended

Timothy's fidelity and, indirectly his mentoring by Lois and Eunice when he wrote: *"But as for you, continue in what you have learned and have firmly believed, knowing from whom you learned it and how from childhood you have been acquainted with the sacred writings which are able to instruct you for salvation through faith in Christ Jesus"* (2 Tim 3:14-15). These two women are affirmed in Scripture not because of Timothy's success in mission, but because they carried out their duties faithfully. They were nurturers of faith who had the vision to allow Timothy to take on his responsibilities and dedicate his life to the ministry for which they had prepared him.

Reflection

At the heart of every woman's spirituality there is a consciousness of the gift of creativity which is a primary characteristic of God our Creator and uniquely distinctive of the female species. The future of the world which came to birth when the Holy Spirit breathed upon the waters of the earth (Gen 1:20-25), and into the nostrils of the first created members of our human race (Gen 2:7), depends on this gift. Central to the fruitfulness of our female creativity is the gift of the Spirit of God quietly at work in the soul. The Spirit moves us to every act of virtue: conception, motherhood, positive relationships, prayer, sensitivity, compassion and enabling.

This gift touches every dimension of life, of faith, of the future of humanity and of the Church. It produces in each of us an intense yearning for relationship, partnership, and outreach in terms of the protection and support of our fellow human beings and our world. These virtues and desires have their roots in scripture. They have been characteristics of women from the time of Sarah in the book of Genesis to Lois and Eunice in the Second Letter of Paul to Timothy; and right down to women such as Catherine McAuley, Foundress of the Sisters of Mercy and her work with the poor and the spiritual formation of women in the nineteenth century; to Dorothy Day, Foundress of the Catholic Worker and her espousal of non-violent action and hospitality to the marginalised in the twentieth century; and to Mother Teresa, Foundress of The Missionaries of Charity and her commitment to the unloved and unwanted together with the dying, or as she liked to say, to "Jesus in disguise", in our own day.

Each of these women lived her life conscious of her partnership with her Creator in continuing to nurture and revitalise the earth, and to ensure the continuation of the human species as a dignified, caring, loving, nurturing, faith-filled and holy people. The initial call to spirituality comes from the Holy Spirit through positive experiences with faith-filled mothers and grandmothers in the formative years. Generally speaking initial spirituality is caught rather than taught. The Holy Spirit having entered the life of the young person at the moment of conception resides quietly in the heart and works silently from there in response to the environment provided in the home situation.

- What key lessons might mothers, in this third millennium, learn in terms of being informed about their faith from Lois and Eunice?

- How did Lois and Eunice embody: (a) the creativity of God? (b) the wisdom of the Holy Spirit?

- How fundamental is the study of Scripture to your faith development and spirituality?

Frequently when I have spoken with teenagers about the Corporal Works of Mercy and the value of sisterly and brotherly out-reach, I have been impressed by their reactions and by their stories of good works practised in their homes by their mothers and grandmothers. They have lived in a situation of quiet and unobtrusive evangelisation. The seed planted by the Holy Spirit and left to germinate has been nurtured. Germination may take place very quickly or it may take years but it will develop in God's time.

Children and teenagers enjoy sharing stories about their virtuous mothers, and increasingly in recent years, of grandmothers whom they have witnessed helping the poor, caring for neighbours' children in times of emergency, sending meals to the sick, visiting hospitals, old people's homes and prisons. Whilst they may appear to distance themselves from such acts, and may not have the language to name the Holy Spirit, they are profoundly affected by having witnessed them. They make mental notes of the goodness which they perceive in others and in the quiet of their own hearts form a desire to be partners in such a value system. In time they identify with positive role models and claim their spirituality as their own.

- Does your parish have a Youth Club, 'Sixteen to Thirty-Somethings,' or Young People's Prayer Group?

- What values might such mentoring gatherings have, if promoted and fostered creatively, in a parish?

At a time when sport was very central in the lives of all young Greek and Greco-Jewish boys and youths, Eunice's husband seems to have decided not to circumcise their son, or to defer the ceremony until the boy became a man. This decision made the young man socially acceptable amongst his Greek peers. It also made possible access to the world of fame more of a realistic option should the boy display potential.

In our day, sport has become something of a god once again. In many families it is an all consuming weekend passion. While children's and young people's thirst for stardom and fame is nurtured and facilitated, their spiritual formation appears to be either neglected or deferred. This is a huge source of concern for Grandmothers and, in some cases, for mothers too.

In order to keep the family unit together and to gain social acceptance, a mother automatically feels obliged to support her husband's and children's desires and ambitions. In itself this is great. However, someone has to take responsibility for faith development, catechesis, spirituality and worship, if these young people are to become integrated and whole people who develop the skills to cope with both success and failure.

- How might parents, club manages and parish clergy set about addressing this issue without either compromising the Sabbath, or further alienating families?

Because of the influences of the media and the current materialistic environment in which most of our young people are raised today, many find the idea of sharing their essentials rather than their surplus unattractive. That is one reason why all of us women and mothers in particular need to be constantly reminding ourselves that actions speak louder than words. We are called to be quietly prayerful, joyfully active, compassionately pastoral and generous in our giving if we are to be truly Spirit-centred in our evangelisation. The days when parents could evangelise their children through preaching, commanding and demanding are long gone, if they ever existed. A focused and meaningful spirituality is, like good example, caught rather than taught.

Experiences such as observing family prayer and the Corporal Works of Mercy being carried out in the home instil values in children and young people and influence how they think and relate to others as they grow into adulthood. These good deeds are part of the spiritual heritage of most women and are to be treasured. They are demonstrations of the practical living out of the Gospel and they are life-giving experiences for those who witness them. Mothers, mother-figures, grandmothers and aunties have it within them, as a free gift of the Holy Spirit, to demonstrate what it means to be a profoundly spiritual person without ever opening a theology book, attending a course or seeking a spiritual guru.

Clearly study and spiritual direction are wonderful helps to those who feel able to make them part of life or to simply indulge in, as little spiritual 'pick-me-ups', from time to time. However, they are not obligatory for genuine sanctity and holistic family living.

- What are the possibilities in (a) your home and (b) your parish or area for young people to develop a practical spirituality?

Some years ago I gave a series of lesson to fourteen year olds on the lives of a selection of female saints. They ranged from Mary the Mother of Jesus to Maria Goretti. I was interested to notice that no young woman who might stand as a chaste role model for post-modern girls had been canonised since 1950!

At the end of the series I set the children a project for independent study. It required them to choose a saint whose life appealed to and challenged them. All of them went to the library to begin their research. Many came back with a selection of books on their chosen saint. Four girls returned quietly and in-dependently with a plea to be allowed to produce a file on their grandmothers and one asked if she could centre her study on her single mother.

Since each child was able to justify her choice in the light of the module of work completed I agreed to the requests. The results were fascinating. I learned far more about the virtues exercised by grandmothers and mothers in terms of creativity, prayer, relation-ship, caring, sensitivity, and enabling than I could expect. It was humbling to see how their children and grandchildren perceived them, and how they reported on their responses to demands, challenges, hardships, abuse inflicted on them and mental anguish endured in silence. Asceticism practised by them and sacrifices endured exceeded much of what I had read in relation to many of the women, and men alike, who had been canonised by Holy Mother Church.

These were women who had lived and continued to live holistic spiritual lives. They were unsophisticated Catholic women who laboured tirelessly in the Lord's vineyard. They had had a profound practical influence on the faith development and spirituality of their grandchildren, their neighbours and their church. I had the joy of welcoming two of the grandmothers and the single mother when the project was completed. The meeting was very moving.

The grandmothers had no concept of how deeply their way of living and being in the world had touched and influenced their grand-daughters. They saw themselves simply as living out their faith commitment and their marriage vows to the best of their abilities. They did not expect to be given flowers for doing what they considered to be their Christian duty. All were delighted that the Holy Spirit's action was bearing fruit in their lives. The single mother was totally unaware of the depth of gratitude felt by her daughter towards her. She did not know that her daughter admired her. They had had what she called, "our moments". There were tears but they were tears of joy and celebration.

- Commitment to what they believed to be the key values in life led Lois and Eunice to nurture Timothy in the faith. What values do you think young mothers and grandmothers spend most time developing in their children and grand-children today?

- List the activities that you spend most of your time on, excluding academic homework, when you are with either your children or grandchildren.

- What proportion of the quality time that you have with your children or young relatives is spent on prayer or matters relating to nurturing a life-giving spirituality?

The saintly monks of old were right in speaking of the purgative way as facilitating spiritual growth. Partnership with the Creator in raising the next generation in the spiritual life is very much a journey from Cana to Calvary. It is only after having navigated this journey that mothers and daughters feel truly free to celebrate, with their foremothers in faith: Sarah, Hannah, Mary, Lois and Eunice at the Resurrection Table.

Prayer

Holy Spirit of God, as mothers and daughters we gather in your presence in gratitude for the gift of faith with which we have been blest. We thank you for our own mothers, who, like Lois and Eunice, treasured their faith and transmitted it to us with love and fidelity. We pray now for all mothers and for all who will become mothers in the future:

Response: [to be said at the end of each grouping]:

"Anoint them with your healing oil of love, peace, mercy and compassion."

Mothers who are rejoicing
Mothers who are pregnant
Mothers who have miscarried a baby
Mothers who are bereaved through the death of a
    cherished daughter
Mothers who have had an abortion and are struggling
    with feelings of guilt
Mothers who are worried about their children
Mothers who are abused or deserted
Mothers who are forced into prostitution
Mothers who are widowed and lonely
Mothers who are suffering from mental illness
Mothers who grieve because they have sons or
    daughters in prison
Mothers who feel crushed because they have lost or
    had a child kidnapped
Mothers who are victims of addiction
Mothers who have had to put their children into care
Mothers who have a child who is an addict
Mothers who have a child suffering from HIV/AIDS
Mothers whose husbands are addicted to drink, other
    drugs or gambling
Mothers who have had a suicide in their family

Response:

We bring before you, Holy Spirit of God, all
    daughters:
Daughters who are struggling with faith issues
Daughters who are lapsed in the practice of their faith

Daughters whose marriages are under strain because of
    infertility
Daughters who are married to men who oppose
    passing on the faith to their children
Daughters who have never had their children baptised
    and who do not teach them to pray
Daughters who are so committed to their jobs and
    social life that they neglect their own mothers
Daughters who devote their lives to doing good works
    at home and on the missions
Daughters who promote the Gospel by their way of
    life and strive to share the faith with others.

Response:

Life-giving Spirit, awaken in all grandmothers,
mothers and daughters a lively spirit of faith, hope,
creativity and love, that they learn the value of living
purposefully, and of sharing and celebrating their faith
in the name of Jesus their Mentor and Saviour. Amen.

NOTES

1   Edith Deen. *All The Women of The Bible.* Harper Collins,
    New York. 1995. p. 238.
2   Deutero-Pauline here refers to the fact that most modern
    scholars do not believe that 1 and 2 Timothy and the letter to
    Titus are the work of Paul. The genre and direction which the
    church seems to be taking does not appear to truly reflect
    Paul's approach.
3   Mary Ann Getty-Sullivan. *Women in the New Testament.* The
    Liturgical Press, Collegeville, Minnesota. 2001. p. 150.
4   Ibid.

5   Robert J Karris, OFM, Gen Edt. The Collegeville Bible
    Commentary. Liturgical Press, Collegeville, Minnesota. 1992.
    p. 1057.
6   Edith Deen. *Wisdom from Women in the Bible.* Harper. San
    Francisco, 1978, 2003. p. 179.
7   Mary Ann Beavis. 2 Thessalonians in *Searching the Scriptures*
    Vol 2. Ed. Elizabeth Schüssler Fiorenza. Crossroads Publ.,
    New York. 1994. p. 264.
8   Mary Ann Getty-Sullivan. *Women in the New Testament.* The
    Liturgical Press, Collegeville, Minnesota. 2001. pp. 152-153.

Priscilla: Listener, Learner and Leader

And he [Paul] found a Jew named Aq'uila, a native of Pontus, lately come from Italy with his wife Priscilla, because Claudius had commanded all the Jews to leave Rome. And he went to see them; and because he was of the same trade he stayed with them, and they worked, for by trade they were tentmakers.   Acts 18:2-3

In relating the story of Paul's Second and Third Missionary Journeys, Luke found himself forced to acknowledge the central role taken in the growth and nurture of the church by Priscilla or Prisca as Paul affectionately called her (Rom 16:3; 1 Cor 16: 19; 2 Tim 4:19).[1] She is seldom mentioned either in Scripture or in scholarship without having her husband Aquila by her side. The church in Rome, Corinth and Ephesus became deeply indebted to them. Priscilla showed herself to be: a keen listener to the promptings of the Holy Spirit (Acts 18:2); willing to learn from Paul and from her experience of life; quick to inculturate her family in the native traditions of her various host nations, without compromising the Gospel (18:18); and fired with a powerful post Pentecost energy for leadership and evangelisation (18:26). As a married couple, she and her husband are also valued for their pastoral care, open communication, generosity, hospitality and discretion. In areas where Paul struggled to form relationships or even failed to get his message across Priscilla and Aquila either rescued him or won the community to the Gospel for him (18:6, 20:1).

Despite the name Priscilla being Latin, its owner was a Jewess from Rome and probably a remnant of the Diaspora. It is most likely that she was converted sometime in the 40s AD in Rome. It is unlikely that her evangelisation took place through Peter as it is believed that when he fled from the house of Mary, the mother of John Mark, he went to Antioch and remained in that region for some considerable time. Priscilla's husband, who came from northern Anatolia or the Pontus Mountain area of present day Turkey was also a relic of one of the many dispersions. He had probably come to Italy with his parents some years before meeting Priscilla in Rome. Their aspiration would have been to find a better life, and to improve and promote their tent-making business.

In contrast to normal convention, Priscilla is often mentioned first in Scripture, and generally thought of in advance of her husband. Scholars explain this by saying that she probably received the faith first, came from a family who were superior to that of Aquila, and that she was academically more accomplished. They are the second married couple to feature prominently in Acts[2]. They present a total contrast to Ananias with his wife Sapphira who, through their own deception, destroyed themselves (5:1-10). Priscilla is often referred to as 'the first Christian evangelist in Rome'. This is because she is thought to have received the gift of faith following the Pentecost experience in Jerusalem. She had engaged in the work of evangelisation before either Peter or Paul arrived in the city of Rome.

Her first convert is thought to have been her husband, Aquila. Scripture tells us, she and her husband were expelled from Rome under an edict of Claudius in 49 AD. The Roman historian Suetonius recorded that the Emperor expelled the Jews from Rome because of their rioting over a person called Chrestus, meaning Christ, as in Christ Jesus the Saviour. The mis-spelling of Christ not only shows that Suetonius was unfamiliar with it, but also, that he did not know the details of the revolt.

The riot was provoked by a Christian group who went around the city proclaiming the Gospel to which the Jews objected. In response the Emperor, who was already under pressure on the boundaries of his empire and not prepared to face trouble in it heart, excluded all recognised Jews and Christians from the city. He did this because the Roman authorities saw Christianity as a sect of Judaism which they viewed with distain. Being Jewish by birth, and a committed Christians in a leading business, and hence in a position of prominence, Priscilla had to leave with her husband under the edict. However, it is most likely that their business and house church, continue under the care of their trusted employees (Rom 16:3-5); because they returned with ease, for a short time in 57 AD.

The pair settled in Corinth and immediately set up a house church in their own home. From this it can be assumed that they had already operated a house church in Rome. Having had difficulties in preaching the Gospel in Athens, Paul arrived in Corinth at about the same time as Priscilla and Aquila

(Acts 17:32-18:1). Initially he was attracted to them because of their faith, Jewishness and the fact that, like himself, they were workers in leather and tent-making. They would have been very impressed by his story of how he came to faith; and the fact that he had been personally commissioned by the Risen Jesus to be an apostle like the original twelve (Acts 9:3-22). They gave him hospitality and found a place for him in their trade so that he could earn his own living while carrying out his missionary work (1 Cor 4:12). Paul always made an effort to be independent of the community in terms of living expenses. It is clear that the twelve and their co-workers were financed by voluntary donations from the faith community (Acts 4:36-37; 1 Cor 9:5).

Tent making was a lucrative business. Although by this time the Jews had become a settled people in the villages, towns and cities of Palestine, Asia Minor and parts of Europe, some continued to invest in tents. They were also popular with travellers, traders and missionaries. Tent making was a highly prized skill. The tents were made from a special strong cloth woven from the hair of goats. Lengths of this cloth were sewn together to form tents which could be either round or oblong in shape. When stretched across carefully positioned poles, and held in place by ropes which were strategically wrapped and knotted around the poles; and then attached to stakes in the ground around the outside, the tents made comfortable dwelling spaces. The way in which they were set up and secured was not dissimilar to how tents are erected on campsites today. Tarsus, from which Paul originated, was known for its superior cloth and skilled craftsmen. Jewish parents took a great pride in teaching the skill to their children.

Priscilla and Aquila worked with Paul in the Corinth mission and so deserve to be seen as his co-founders in that mission. Archaeologists have established that a house church such as Priscilla's and Aquila's would have been large enough to house twenty to forty people and that the courtyard would have been able to house many, many more. From this it is fair to suggest that the community at Corinth for which they took responsibility increased rapidly. Community worship was celebrated in their house. There too, catechesis and prayers took place. During his free time, Paul concentrated on preaching in the Synagogue against harsh opposition from some Jews who eventually forced him out. *"And when they opposed and reviled him, he shook out his garments and said to them, "Your blood be upon your heads! I am innocent. From now on I will go to the Gentiles"* (18:6). With the support of Priscilla and Aquila, he rented a house next door to the synagogue and there made many converts amongst the Gentiles.

Paul spent eighteen months in partnership ministry with Priscilla and her husband during this first visit to Corinth. They taught the Word of God among the people despite continuing opposition from the Jews who even brought charges of provocation against him before the tribunal. However, the pro-Counsel cleared him saying: *"If it were a matter of wrongdoing or vicious crime, I should have reason to bear with you, O Jews; but since it is a matter of questions about words and names and your own law, see to it yourselves; I refuse to be a judge of these things"* (18:14b-16). He then drove the Jews from the tribunal.

Despite Paul being cleared of any wrong doing, he began to feel that God had other work for him and for Priscilla and Aquila. However, they continued to minister in Corinth for a little longer while they made arrangements for the management of their business interests, waited for good weather conditions and suitable spring tides. Scripture does not tell us who took continuing charge of the church in Corinth. However, we know that Silas and Timothy had already arrived there in support of the mission (18:5); and that following Priscilla's evangelising efforts, support was sent from Ephesus some time later (19:1).

In addition to this, we know from Paul's on-going communication with the Corinthian church, by letter, that a female disciple called Chloe, who was a trusted confidant of Paul, held a position of leadership there with Paul's blessing: *"For it has been reported to me by Chloe's people that there is quarrelling among you, my brethren"* (1 Cor 1:11). Little is known of Chloe. But Paul makes it abundantly clear that she was a recognised and respected leader of a house church. It is quite possible that she had been an employee of Priscilla's and Aquila's. In that case she would have been an ideal manageress for the business and leader of the house church in their absence.

Back at sea again Priscilla and her companions travelled two hundred and fifty miles across the Aegean Sea to found a new mission in the thriving city of Ephesus.[3] This journey took them ten days and gave them time to reflect on political dangers and to prepare their mission strategies and plans. Ephesus, situated three miles from the shore on the River Cayster, was the fourth largest city in the

Roman Empire and a centre steeped in the worship of idols. It had its own twenty-four-thousand-seater amphitheatre. Within two miles, to the north of the city centre stood the renowned Temple of Artemis, which was regarded as one of the Seven Wonders of the World. The missionaries found that there were a number of Christians at various stages in the evangelisation process, already resident in the city.

Priscilla and her husband set up a new satellite of their business there. Once again, they opened a house church and became a centre for the faith community, as is made clear by Paul in his First Letter to Corinth, which scholars believe was written from Ephesus: *"The churches of Asia send greetings. Aq'uila and Prisca, together with the church in their house, send you hearty greetings in the Lord"* (1 Cor 16:19). When Paul left Ephesus for Jerusalem shortly after arriving in the city, Priscilla and her husband took over his apostolic work in the synagogues.

There they met Apollos, who had taken up a preaching position: "He had been instructed in the way of the Lord; and being fervent in spirit, he spoke and taught accurately the things concerning Jesus, though he knew only the baptism of John" (Acts 18:25). Priscilla showed her diplomatic, and pastoral skills at their best, when, instead of challenging him in public, she took him aside and with the support of her husband, introduced him to baptism in Jesus and demonstrated to him that Jesus was indeed the fulfilment of the Promise[4] and the Saviour of the world (Gen 12:3; Gal 3:16). Apollos stayed with the couple for a short time. When he expressed a desire to move on to Achaia which took in Corinth, they supported him:

And when he wished to cross to Acha'ia, the brethren encouraged him, and wrote to the disciples to receive him. When he arrived, he greatly helped those who through grace had believed, for he powerfully confuted the Jews in public, showing by the scriptures that the Christ was Jesus.

Acts 18:27-28

The Gospel was always Priscilla's priority. In releasing and indeed, in promoting Apollos by sending a letter of support to the church in Achaia, she was displaying her altruism and that of her husband. Additionally, she was demonstrating her ability to delegate leadership to others and to trust newly evangelised members to be faithful to the Good News. Her trust was repaid as verified by Paul when he called him *"our brother"*, meaning that he accepted him as having received adequate catechesis and being unconditionally committed to the mission of Jesus: *"As for our brother Apol'los, I strongly urged him to visit you with the other brethren, but it was not at all his will to come now. He will come when he has opportunity"* (1 Cor 16:12).

In this statement, Paul was also saying that he loved and respected Apollos, and that he, as co-founder of the church in Corinth with Priscilla and her husband, wanted him to visit the community and make a contribution to the on-going and expanding mission there. This invitation from Paul to Apollos is a further affirmation, by the apostle, of the successful evangelising skills of Priscilla. It also enables scholars to assert authoritatively that she, in partnership with Aquila, had become the 'mother' who led Apollos to the fullness of the Christian faith and gave him his new credentials for mission. That

173

Apollos' name is mentioned ten times in Scripture is a demonstration of his centrality in the work of evangelisation and his contribution to the ever expanding mission in Greece and throughout Asia Minor.

In his weekly address to a general audience gathered in St Peter's Square in Rome on 7 February 2007, Pope Benedict XVI, cited Priscilla and her husband as a "married couple [who] played a very active role in the post-Paschal origins of the Church." He went on to define their role in Ephesus as: "welcoming into their house the group of local Christians when gathered to listen to the Word of God, and to celebrate the Eucharist. It is exactly this type of gathering that in Greek is called 'ekklesia' ... which means convocation, assembly, gathering." Here the Holy Father has used the word Eucharist but has not indicated who presided at the sacred ritual. It seems reasonable to assume that since the house belonged to Priscilla and Aquila who were respected as leaders and acted as hosts, they also assumed the roles of presiders.

The Holy Father went on to point out that a similar pattern for worship was, according to Paul, followed later at Corinth, where the then president was Gaius, Paul's host (Rom 16:23). The pattern was repeated in Laodicea, where the local faith community met in the home of Nympha (Col 4:15). Little is known of Nympha apart from the fact that like Chloe at Corinth, she led a house church in Laodicea which was about ten and half miles west of Colossae and ninety-nine and a half miles east of Ephesus. Nympha is the only leader mentioned by name in Laodicea, so it seems reasonable to assume that she, like Priscilla and Aquila, presided at Eucharist in her house church. She may have been one of the group of twelve on whom Paul *'laid his hands'* at Ephesus, during his Third Missionary Journey (19:1-10). It is most likely that being a friend of Paul's, she became known to Priscilla and Aquila. She may even have shared ministry with them at some time in Asia. It is interesting that His Holiness, mentions her when speaking about Priscilla and her husband.

Paul eventually returned and joined Priscilla and Aquila again in ministry in Ephesus. Although a gifted and dedicated missionary, he does not appear to have been blest with either the pastoral or diplomatic skills of Priscilla. In his enthusiasm for the truth, he quickly caused considerable unrest by holding a public burning of scrolls dedicated to the magic arts. "Ephesus was a centre for magical arts, and the scrolls were of considerable value."[5] He went on to create further disquiet when he criticised the worship of false gods, and replicas of the goddess Artemis created and sold by the silversmith Demetrius (19:23 ff). Fear that this preaching would loose Demetrius his income and his employees their jobs, led to a riot in the city. Thanks to the quick response of his friends, amongst whom are thought to have been Priscilla and Aquila, Paul was rescued and encouraged to leave the area, despite the fact that once again he was cleared of any wrong doing by the authorities. Yet again Priscilla and Aquila were the pourers of oil on troubled waters.

In his Letter to the Romans Paul writes: *"Greet Prisca and Aq'uila, my fellow workers in Christ Jesus, who risked their necks for my life, to whom not only I but also all the churches of the Gentiles give thanks"* (Rom 16:3-4). Scholars believe that the statement of indebtedness here refers to the episode with Demetrius in Ephesus. Pope Benedict, continuing his address, comments in reference to this statement: "What extraordinary praise for these two married persons … And it is none other than Paul who extends it. He explicitly recognises in them two true and important collaborators of his apostolate." Commenting on Priscilla's place in a male dominated society and Scripture, Gail O'Day writes:

> "Paul's high assessment of Priscilla and other women leaders runs contrary to Luke's own more ambivalent assessment of women's leadership… Luke never identifies the work of Priscilla and Aquila as ministry, but his description of what they do, leaves no doubt Priscilla was a missionary and a teacher… Luke studiously avoided discussing women's leadership, but he could not avoid this subject in the story of Priscilla because she was too well known. He did try, however, to tell her story with as much restraint and decorum as possible."[6]

While this is true of Acts, its readers need to be conscious of the audience and purpose for which it was intended; and the symbolism of twelve men in leadership to both Jews and Romans (Acts 1:1-13). In contrast to O'Day's analysis, Clarice Marin, comments that Acts presents Priscilla as "a woman exercising decisive leadership and sustained intellectual engagement and instruction with a male who was himself an *"eloquent man, well-versed in the scriptures"* (Acts 18:24). She is not subordinate to Aquila, nor is she preoccupied with domestic duties!"[7]

Commenting on the value of lay people such as Priscilla and her husband during the address mentioned above, the Holy Father went on:

> "This couple in particular demonstrates how important the action of Christian spouses is. When they are supported by faith and by a strong spirituality, their courageous commitment for the Church and in the Church becomes natural. The daily sharing of their life prolongs and in some way is sublimated in the assuming of a common responsibility in favour of the Mystical Body of Christ, even if just a little part of it. Thus it was in the first generation and thus it will often be."

It is wonderful to know that the Holy Father sees Pricilla and her husband as such powerful pillars in the early church. It good to know too, that he is certainly not ignoring, overlooking or under valuing the 'priesthood of the people' of God, and their giftedness in supporting one another on life's pilgrimage. This statement is a fine accolade to Priscilla and Aquila and indeed to all married couples in ministry who devote themselves faithfully to the Christian calling which is to holiness of life following the model set by Priscilla and Aquila.

When the Emperor Claudius died having been poisoned by his second wife in 54 AD, he was succeeded by his seventeen-year-old step-son Nero who rescinded the edict of 49 AD. This allowed Priscilla and Aquila, together with many other

Christian and Jewish business people, to return to Rome. In their absence the church and their business were nurtured by their co-workers The return enabled them to make innovations in their business in the light of their experiences in Asia and the developing markets in parts of south Eastern Europe. The move gave them an opportunity to affirm members of this house church who continued to be faithful. Having completed their business, yet again they demonstrated the virtue of detachment and their skills in delegation, by leaving their delegates to carry on the work in Rome while they returned to the younger and more insecure mission in Ephesus. In the Deutero-Pauline Second Letter to Timothy greetings are sent from Paul to Prisca (Priscilla) and her husband, who scholars believe, are back in ministry in Ephesus (2 Tim 4:19).

The fact that Priscilla was a married woman could have enhanced her value as a role model in the changing and developing church that is reflected in the three Deutero-Pauline Pastoral Letters, the genre and teaching content of which are considerably different from Paul's letters hitherto. At the time in which these later letters were written the church was having problems in terms of lack of educated women, and undesirable interpersonal relationships between the genders. Women were beginning to be portrayed as gullible because of their lack of formal learning (1 Tim 2:11-15). For these reasons amongst others relating to celibacy, and the perceived 'vulnerability' of men; the writer of this letter felt it necessary to recommend restricting women to domestic life and to teaching within female circles. In the light of this argument, it was essential to present the faith community with an authentic missionary woman who had proved that she could not only manage her marital relationship, but use it for the good of the church, and engage in teaching the male gender fruitfully.

She stood out as a paradigm of virtue, learning, prudence, sound faith and diplomacy. In a partnership of love and fidelity, she had demonstrated in Rome, Corinth and Ephesus that women who are educated and understand the Scriptures make excellent teachers, wives, missionaries and co-workers in ministry. Well informed church leaders such as Apollos, Timothy and Barnabas would have had considerable difficulty in digesting the Deutero-Pauline advice. "If the later (Deutero-Pauline) restrictions against women's "teaching" had applied to Prisca, then Apollos and Paul, as well as the "rest of the Gentile Churches" would have been missing a vital, well-educated, and apparently very well-loved Christian model."[8]

REFLECTION

As a post Pentecost couple the enthusiasm shown by Priscilla and Aquila for the Gospel is inspiring. In our Church nowadays, this passion is often much more noticeable in recent converts than it is in cradle Catholics. It presents a challenge to us and it invites us to reflect on our own commitment to the Gospel and our response to the command: *"Go therefore and make disciples of all nations, baptizing them in the name of the Father and of the Son and of the Holy Spirit, teaching them to observe all that I have commanded you; and lo, I am with you always, to the close of the age"* (Mt 28:19-20). In addition to that it invites us to consider the value which we place on those brothers and sisters who join our faith communities at the Easter Vigil each year.

In some parts of the United States parishioners have a practice of going to the house of new neighbours and offering them a loaf of bread. They also make a point of inviting them for coffee or a drink in their homes as part of helping them to settle in and get to know their neighbours. This is a touching and very simple way of being Christian and of breaking bread with or being Eucharist to new neighbours, regardless of their creed, social status or ethnicity.

- How welcoming are you to new members joining your parish be they cradle Catholics who have arrived from another area or country; or who joined your community within the last two to three years?

- As a post Pentecost Christian what contribution do you, personally, make to neighbourliness, in terms of offering hospitality, a place in ministry or an invitation to a prayer group, society or guild?

Having established a church in Corinth, Priscilla and Aquila entrusted it to others giving them the freedom to develop it and where necessary and appropriate to introduce innovations. Such an approach displayed trust, purity of intention in ministry on their part in the sense that they did not try to control it as their 'baby'. It was their 'baby' but like all good parents, their only desire was that it should grow healthy and strong. In handing it over, they demonstrate the virtue of detachment to us.

This is a virtue in which many of us need educating in these days of diminishing numbers of practising Catholics. We need to ask ourselves if, in the honesty of our hearts, we can say that we not only make room for the young, the new and the inexperienced in ministry; but actually encourage them to share their experiences of being and of living church.

- Are there times when you feel threatened by new community members?

- Do you sometimes long to be relieved of a particular ministry in your parish, and yet, when a possible volunteer appears on the horizon, feel a new urge to hold on to it?

- Do you sometimes tell yourself and others that you are only clinging on to your Communion Ministry 'because there is no one else to do it', when in fact, you have never tested the community?

There is a story told of a religious community which was having problems with one of its members who was 'a controller'. The man's enthusiasm for mission had been great at one stage in his life and he had achieved a remarkable amount. However his achievements had become strictly his and those of his 'dependent'. Between them they managed to make life hard for their brothers and without knowing it, they did likewise for those in ministry with them. One day the Provincial arrived and sought the confidential advice of the community on how he might help the two men and in helping them, re-energise the community and re-activate and expand the mission. On being told that it might be helpful to move, at least one of the pair to another community, he replied: "Oh, I could not possibly do that as the mission would fall apart." What a reflection on the entire Order? What a death sentence to the community and part of its holistic mission? What a lack of energy, creatively and life-giving vision for the future of the Order and the Gospel?

That the mission was already severely restricted, in need of a boost and possibly a change of direction had either evaded him; or he was too scared of 'the controller' to act in the way that he knew to be right in terms of creating unity and furthering the reign of God.

Priscilla and her co-workers were in ministry for the sake of the Gospel and they never allowed that small letter 'i' in ministry to become the capital 'I' as in, I'm important or, 'It's mine'.

- Can you think of any area in your parish life, family life, ministry or business relationships where an insatiable desie for control is limiting new initiatives and the power of the Good News?

When Paul confronted Demetrius, he was confronting a controller, a manipulator and a man who focused on material wealth alone. Paul paid the price for his intervention. However, he did make an impression. In doing so he at least tried to give the Gospel a hope of breathing and taking life in threatening territory.

In our day the local drug pusher is the Demetrius of Ephesus. Cocaine and alcohol are the cuisine and Champagne on which many of our young and middle aged community members feast on Saturday nights in a search for status, comfort and relaxation. On Sunday mornings, instead of joining the community in worship, or enjoying quality family time, they crouch over sinks, or curl up on their couches like screwed up zombies. Our 'poor little rich world' needs a new Priscilla who will listen to the Holy Spirit, read the signs of the times, and then, move in with the only cuisine and Champagne that bring peace, power over self, and comfort: the Good News and the Eucharist.

- Are there any strategies, or support services in place in your community to help parents who worry about the danger of cocaine becoming a 'companion' to one of their children?

- Is there a danger that some parents in your parish are willing hosts to the cocaine culture?

Ephesus became the chief centre of Christianity during the early days of the church. In our day, and despite the intense evangelising strategies employed by Islam, the city has a population of thirty thousand Christians. Speaking in 2006 in advance of Pope Benedict XVI's visit to Turkey and the city of Ephesus in particular, Cardinal Ignace Moussa Daoud, the Vatican Prefect for the Congregation of Eastern Churches, said that Turkey is "the cradle of Christianity ...a privileged place for the implementation of Christianity ... [that saw] the flowering of theologies and of rites." Out of this has grown the wonderful mosaic of Christianity we know in our day. This is part of the on-going harvest being reaped because of the versatility, creativity and life-giving ministry exercised there nearly two thousand years ago by Pricilla, her husband and their co-workers.

Commenting on the development of the emerging Church, Pope Benedict XVI said: "One thing is sure: together with the gratitude of the early Church, of which St Paul speaks, we must also add our own, since thanks to the faith and apostolic commitment of the lay faithful, of families, of spouses like Priscilla and Aquila, Christianity has reached our generation."

- Priscilla and Aquila left Corinth at the request of Paul in order to bring the Gospel to another nation. What practical contribution do you or your parish make to the proclamation of the Good News in far-off lands today?

- In our current Church there has been a dearth of vocations to the Consecrated Life and to the Ordained Ministry for some years. It is now reaching crisis point. Might the Holy Spirit be inviting us to reflection and or action in some new way?

- Much has been written in recent years about a need to 'return to the charism of the founder' and the roots of religious life or Congregations in the Church. Might this invitation need to be extended to a wider audience in relation to the original Founder of the Christian community?

- Are you and your parish aware that if the Gospel is to flourish in the future, priests and religious must be called forth from the benches in your own parish church?

Priscilla and Aquila were a caring, pastoral and empathetic couple who took Apollos aside discretely and completed his evangelisation. They did not challenge him in public; display their superior knowledge for everyone present to hear, or degrade him in any way. They sensed the faith that had already been planted deep in his heart and that was awaiting enlightenment. It was they, in partnership with the Holy Spirit who gave him the power and the knowledge to refute the Jews and demonstrate that Jesus was indeed the Saviour (Acts 18:27-28).

They had learned a lesson from Jesus' dealings with people such as the women taken in adultery (Jn 8:3-12). They recognised a mistake, an error and ignorance when they saw and heard it. However, they helped to put the wrong right using Gospel skills as opposed to those of heathen orators.

- When we are blest with the perception to see 'a speck' in our sister's or brother's eye (Mt 7:3), at whatever level in the faith community today, what course of action do we take?

- How charitable are we when we hear gossip about other couples in our parish or when we hear of some misdemeanour committed by one of their children?

Priscilla and Aquila are always mentioned together in Scripture. Theirs seems to have been an ideal marriage. Perhaps the secret rested in that they always kept God at the centre of their relationship, and nurtured their life together by prayer and Eucharist. To them marriage was a divine institution, a reflection of the Trinity. They were a true partnership and a source of nourishment for each other. In the image of the first family at Nazareth they lived and worked together for each other; and like the first family who formed the first church, they made their home their church also. That was their sacred space, place of relaxation, sharing, Scripture study and quiet reflection.

Their Scriptures never needed to be dusted. They were used daily and with reverence. In times of difficulty and misunderstanding they knew the value of forgiveness. They knew how to share their joys and their sorrows. Being a human pair, they had their share of problems and there must have been times when Paul's unique communication skills challenged them and created tension between them. Yet they managed to persevere, possibly because they knew that anything that is worth having is worth working for. In addition to that they kept themselves focused on ministry, on helping others, on developing their business and on the Good News.

- In recent years even the 'very best' of Christian couples seem to find marriage a challenge. Discuss some of the possible reasons for this.

- Might there be areas in which women and men in the third millennium could learn something about Christian marriage and fidelity to an unconditional commitment from this early Christian couple?

- If you had to give advice to a young couple preparing for marriage today what might you say to them?

- Where is your sacred space? How often does your Bible need to be dusted or do you even know where your Sacred Scripture is in your home?

Prayer

Gracious and Loving God, we come before you to celebrate the giftedness of Priscilla. We praise you for the wonders you worked through her in partnership with her husband and co-workers. We praise you too, for their fidelity to each other and the great example that they have put before us of a happy and fulfilled married, and faith filled life.

We pray for all married couples. We give thanks for those who support each other lovingly, and who see their relationship as an unconditional commitment made in love.

We pray, too, for those who make the mistake of putting, sport, peers and business before family; and when under stress, struggle with fidelity. Give them the grace to get their priorities right. Teach them the arts of prioritising, sharing, and making quality time for each other.

We remember all the married couples who have been so devoted to witnessing to the Good News down through the millennia. Your presence within them enabled them to claim and use their natural strength in service; to take risks like Paul; to uproot and move on to areas of new need like Priscilla and Aquila; and to reach out in mercy, love and compassion in your name.

In our day, give us the wisdom of your Spirit, the empathy of your Son, and the creativity of your touch, so that we may, as individuals, families and groups bring healing to our own lives, homes and world, and so bring your reign to fulfilment. Amen.

NOTES

1   Gail R. O'Day. "Acts" in *Women's Bible Commentary*, Eds. Carol A. Newsom and Sharon H Ringe. Westminster John Knox Press, Louisville, Kentucky. 1998. p. 398.

2   Clarice J. Martin. The Acts of the Apostles in *Searching the Scriptures*, Vol 2. Ed. Elizabeth Schüssler Fiorenza. Crossroads Publ. New York. 1994. p. 785.

3   Joanne Turpin. *Twelve Apostolic Women.* St Anthony Messenger Press, Cincinnati, Ohio. 2004. p. 84.

4   *Catechism of the Catholic Church.* Geoffrey Chapman, London. Revised Edition 1999. p 163, ¶ 706.

5   Joanne Turpin. *Twelve Apostolic Women.* St Anthony Messenger Press, Cincinnati, Ohio. 2004. p. 85.

6   Gail R. O'Day. "Acts" in *Women's Bible Commentary*, Eds. Carol A. Newsom and Sharon H Ringe. Westminster John Knox Press, Louisville, Kentucky. 1998. p. 400.

7   Clarice J. Martin, The Acts of the Apostles in *Searching the Scriptures* Vol 2. Ed. Elizabeth Schüssler Fiorenza. Crossroads Publ., New York. 1994. p. 785.

8   Mary Ann Getty-Sullivan. *Women in the New Testament.* The Liturgical Press, Collegeville, Minnesota. 2001. p. 161.

Phoebe: Deacon, Daughter
and Delegate

*I commend to you our sister Phoebe, a deaconess
[diakonos] of the church at Cen'chre-ae, that you
may receive her in the Lord as befits the saints,
and help her in whatever she may require from
you, for she has been a helper [prostatis] of many
and of myself as well.* Rom 16:1-2

This statement from the lips of Paul, in recommendation and affirmation of Phoebe, makes clear
to us that gender equality in ministry was a characteristic of the post Pentecost Pauline, church. However,
his inclusion of the words *diakonos and prostatis*, in
recommending Phoebe to the Romans; and 'apostle'
in relation to Junia, in the same chapter (16:7),
presents huge challenges to androcentric translators
of the Letter to the Romans.

When thought of in terms of our contemporary
situation, the two very important verses quoted above
raise more questions than they answer. "Phoebe is
best known today, not for her contributions as
patron, minister, evangelist and all-round benefactor
but, for the debate engendered by the title given
in Paul's letter."[1] An in-depth analysis of Paul's
recommendation of this dynamic and multi-skilled
missionary in concert with his greetings to Junia and
other named women in Rome would demand an

189

entire tome. That is a work for another time and context.

A number of scholars, who critique Paul's Letter to the Romans, avoid having to pronounce on Phoebe's ministry as a deacon (*diakonos*) and leader (*prostatis*) using a variety of arguments. Some state that chapter sixteen is only an attachment to the original letter, which Coleridge described as "...the most profound work in existence". These justify their stance by saying that in chapter sixteen: Paul changes his tenor and moves from teacher to affirming and grateful friend; from theology to history; and from the general to the specific. Others point out that in some original manuscripts, the conclusion of the chapter:

> *Now to him who is able to strengthen you according to my gospel and the preaching of Jesus Christ, according to the revelation of the mystery which was kept secret for long ages but is now disclosed and through the prophetic writings is made known to all nations, according to the command of the eternal God, to bring about the obedience of faith – to the only wise God be glory for evermore through Jesus Christ! Amen.* 16:25-27

is a reflection of two possible conclusions in chapter 15:13 and 15:30-33. This, they argue indicates that the letter which is a summary of Paul's teaching was possibly intended for wider use, possibly as in a circular to various communities; and that they received it minus chapter sixteen, which was a later 'cover letter' for Rome alone. They also maintain that some of the greetings contained in the chapter are possibly too personal when offered by Paul to a group of missionaries who may have been known to him; but are now members of a church which was not one of his foundations, and which he has never visited (16:3-16). They ignore Paul's great desire to make clear that he has had a strong personal relationship with members who though now in Rome, had served elsewhere on mission with him in the past; and his need, now, to regain their patronage for his proposed mission to evangelise the peoples of Spain (Rom 15:24).

However, contemporary research generally supports the chapter as an integral part of Paul's Letter to the church in Rome, bearing in mind, amongst other points, that without it, "Rom 1-15, would be the sole letter in the Pauline corpus to lack an epistolary ending,[2] and that the letter is formally addressed to the church in Rome: *"To all God's beloved in Rome, who are called to be saints: Grace to you and peace from God our Father and the Lord Jesus Christ"* (1:7). "The very significant, if still sketchy, glimpse into the rich life of the early Church, including the leadership of women seen there, ought not to be relegated to a peripheral subchapter just because such roles cannot be imagined by some interpreters."[3]

The founder of the Roman church to which Phoebe was sent as Paul's delegate is unknown. Its roots in the faith were probably set by women and men who were visitors from Rome to Jerusalem on that first Pentecost Sunday when Peter spoke to the assembly after receiving the Holy Spirit:

Now there were dwelling in Jerusalem Jews, devout men from every nation under heaven. And at this sound the multitude came together, and they were bewildered, because each one heard them speaking in his own language. And they were amazed and wondered, saying, "Are not all these who are speaking Galileans? And how is it that we hear, each of us in his own native language? Par'thians and Medes and E'lamites and residents of Mesopota'mia, Judea and Cappado'cia, Pontus and Asia, Phryg'ia and Pamphyl'ia, Egypt and the parts of Libya belonging to Cyre'ne, and visitors from Rome, both Jews and proselytes, Cretans and Arabians, we hear them telling in our own tongues the mighty works of God... But Peter, standing with the eleven, lifted up his voice and addressed them, "Men of Judea and all who dwell in Jerusalem, let this be known to you, and give ear to my words..." And Peter said to them, "Repent, and be baptized every one of you in the name of Jesus Christ for the forgiveness of your sins; and you shall receive the gift of the Holy Spirit. For the promise is to you and to your children and to all that are far off, every one whom the Lord our God calls to him." And he testified with many other words and exhorted them, saying, "Save yourselves from this crooked generation." So those who received his word were baptized, and there were added that day about three thousand souls.

Acts 2:5-11,14; 38-41

The Church was certainly very much alive in Rome in 57 AD, despite Agrippa having had the Apostle James killed in 42 AD (Acts 12:2); Claudius having banished all leading Jews and Christians in 49 AD (Acts 18:2), and Nero only having allowed them back in 54 AD. By the time Phoebe arrived there in 57 AD, none of the apostles had yet set foot in Rome. Paul had planned to do so but never managed to make the journey. Despite all of this, he knew from his contacts that the church was vibrant.

That was the community to which Phoebe carried Paul's letter in about 57 AD. It had been his earnest desire to get there himself for some time; but he had been prevented from doing so (1:11-13). As his ambassador, she was laying the foundation for his visit (15:24; 31-32). This she would do through delivering the letter to the leaders of the community and possibly reading it with them before they presented it to their communities when they gathered for worship. In typical Pauline fashion the Letter is anchored in the Old Testament in order to demonstrate continuity and fulfilment. It is Paul's introduction of himself, his theology, doctrine, and pastoral approach in his role *"as a servant of Jesus Christ, called to be an apostle, set apart for the gospel of God..."* (1:1). Its carrier was a seasoned leader, evangeliser, traveller and business diplomat.

Phoebe was a true daughter of the Holy Spirit. She was not afraid to go to foreign or dangerous places for the sake of the Gospel. Her story is irrefutable proof that single women were as Spirit-filled and as fearless in travelling abroad in the role of apostles and evangelisers as were men such as Paul, Barnabas, Silas and Timothy. She has the honour of being the only named Christian disciple in Cenchreae. Naming in Scripture is seen as a sign that the person was widely approved of, valued and affirmed. Phoebe would have been conscious of this as she made the eight hundred mile journey from Cenchreae, an international port seven miles east of Corinth, to Rome, the Imperial City and the heart of the Roman Empire.

She was a lone female missionary journeying with an energy that could only be described as Pentecostal. It is thought that she travelled by land as far as possible and then joined a caravan group. Her route would have been north through Achaia and Macedonia, and across the narrow Sea of Adria, the modern Adriatic, into Italy. She would have completed her journey by land to Rome. On the way north she would have stopped off at various little Christian enclaves to pray, share Eucharist with and affirm the communities for the commitment to the faith and to on-going evangelisation.

Paul had no hesitation is describing her as a *'diakonos'*. Grammatically this is a masculine term and used in the New Revised Standard Version of the Bible (NRSV). Some translators feminise it as deaconess as in the Jerusalem Bible. This may have been done as a gesture of respect for her gender or it may be an attempt to describe a role inferior to that fulfilled by men. Others such as the New American Bible use the word minister. This is thought by some to be more gender neutral and generic. There is no indication that Paul imaged Phoebe as in any way taking a lesser role in ministry than her male counterparts.[4] However, androcentric translators have a need to portray Phoebe's role as subordinate.

These men appear to forget that in some manuscripts, that record accounts of the commissioning of Timothy by Paul, similar language is used. For example some say: *"our brother and diakonos of God"* meaning deacon; while others state: *"our brother and 'synergos' of God"*, meaning co-worker. The word *diakonos* appears to be a major source of conflict between some androcentric and gynocentric translators. Regardless of how this issue is resolved, it seems clear that Phoebe carried out the same role and ministry in Rome as Timothy and Titus did in Corinth and Thessalonica. As Getty-Sullivan points out, Phoebe had a more responsible role.[5] She was the first formally delegated and commissioned missionary to take the fullness of the Gospel to the heart of the Empire. Her role was, therefore, greater than that of her male co-workers who were visitors to churches in which Paul had already served. Paul's use of the word *diakonos* establishes definitely that women were not seen simply as subordinates to men in ministry. They were commissioned and accepted as independent, authentic and trustworthy leaders in witness, proclamation and nurture.

It is easy to accept that in view of the models and cultural influences at work during the time of Luke's writing of Acts, he had to portray leadership in the emerging church as following the familiar pattern being exercised in Jerusalem and in Rome, if he was to win men in leadership positions to the Gospel. However, Paul was ministering to a totally different culture in a different country twenty years before Luke wrote his work. He rightly exercised a form of leadership in ministry that fitted in with the culture of the host nation as is clear in his partnership ministry in Philippi (Acts 16:14-15,40); Ephesus (18:18-26); and Colossae (Col 4:15). Inculturation had become a reality in these multicultural and multi-racial cities and the Good News was flourishing, despite Jewish and Roman efforts to control, discriminate and restrict the work of the Holy Spirit.

The word *prostatis* as used by Paul in describing Phoebe is the second major issue with certain scholars simply because he applied it to a woman. It is generally translated as leader, president, patron, chief, protector or guardian. According to Paul this was an appropriate word to use in outlining Phoebe's credentials. Some academics go to great pains to explain away any leadership roles or offices which Phoebe may have fulfilled. This is probably done in deference to Jewish, Roman, and later developments in Christian Church Leadership.

Ernst Käsemann goes so far as to say: "Women could not take on legal function, and according to Revelation only in heretical circles do prophetesses seem to have had official ecclesiastical powers of leadership …The idea is that of personal care which Paul and others have received at the hands of the deaconess."[6] He neglects to give evidence for such a biased statement; and to acknowledge that there were other western and eastern cultures with models of leadership which contrasted with that of Rome and Palestine, and were equally effective for their peoples. In addition to this he ignores the fact that the church, operating under some of these gender inclusive leaderships was spreading rapidly in multicultural cities such as Philippi, Ephesus, Corinth, and Thessalonica. In these cities church membership offered women and men equal respect, authority and freedom in leadership.

Like many of her female colleagues in ministry, Phoebe is thought to have come from a wealthy background, to have been well educated, and to have gained excellent leadership and diplomatic skills through business and travel. Unlike many of the other women mentioned in the New Testament, she like Lydia is mentioned in her own right. So well established is she in business and in the faith community that there is no need to refer to her in terms of a male relative. Paul treasured her as a versatile and dynamic missionary who was faithful to the Gospel and a compassionate carer to God's people. He was not concerned about gender, human positions or earthly power. He was totally focused on the Gospel which assured salvation through Jesus Christ.

In the letter which he had entrusted to Phoebe, he sent greetings to twenty six people by name, ten of whom were women. Amongst these was a woman named Junia who had previously been imprisoned with her husband and Paul for her evangelising activities: *"Greet Androni'cus and Ju'nias, my kinsmen and my fellow prisoners; they are men of note among the apostles, and they were in Christ before me"* (16:7). In this we have the third challenge faced by androcentric translators. Some have felt obliged to resort to gender-change. Paul actually used the female name Junia, but interpreters have altered that to the male Ju'nias in an effort to eliminate the idea that a woman could possibly fulfil the role of an apostle. It is possible that they are motivated by a certain respect for the role fulfilled by 'the twelve' in ministry with Jesus: *"And he appointed twelve, to be with him, and to be sent out to preach..."* (Mt 3:4). However, it is noticeable in the New Testament that the necessity for twelve which was so essential to the apostles after the death of Judas (Acts 1:15-26), disappeared with the execution of James by Agrippa in 42 AD.

Thankfully, the New Revised Standard Version, which is generally respected as the most authentic translation, in these islands, records her name accurately: *"Greet Andronicus and Junia, my relatives who were in prison with me; they are prominent among the apostles, and were in Christ before I was"* (16:7). In commenting on androcentric reaction against the idea that a woman could possibly be called an apostle, Elizabeth A. Castelli writes: "Once again, the argument is a circular syllogism: since by definition, women cannot be apostles, when a woman is called an apostle, she is either not an apostle or she is not a woman".[7]

It is possible that Junia and her husband were in Jerusalem on Pentecost Sunday, and received both the news of the Risen Jesus and Baptism from Peter (Acts 2:22-41). It is most likely that they made a distinct contribution to the foundation of the church in Rome after Pentecost; and that they continued to nurture it in some way despite having been in prison for a short time. It was a custom in the early church that missionaries stay as guests with known leaders when they were visiting in new areas. In light of this it is reasonable to believe that Phoebe spent time with Junia and her husband while in Rome. They would have been key leaders in making sure Paul's teaching was heard, understood and assimilated by the church in Rome.

On completing her mission, Phoebe would have returned home to report to Paul and to resume her duties as leader, benefactor *and "deaconess of the church at Cen'chre-ae"* (16:1). St John Chrysostom praised

Phoebe as an inspiration, and a model for both genders to emulate in ministry. He described her as a saint and a woman who served the church in the office of deacon. She is often cited as a paradigm to be imitated in compassionate caring, witness and proclamation. Some scholars suggest that she is a fitting prototype for women deacons in the same way as Stephen (Acts 6:5), is portrayed as a model for men. In our day, she is revered as a saint by the Lutheran Church in the United States of America and her feast is celebrated on 27th January.

REFLECTION

The earliest Christian use of the term *diakonos* occurs in: *"Paul and Timothy, servants of Christ Jesus, to all the saints in Christ Jesus who are at Philip'pi, with the bishops and deacons..."* (Phil 1:1). No 'job description' is given; but the impression gained is that they were helpers to the bishops in ministry. When Christians hear the term deacon today they generally think of it in relation to the seven men appointed by the disciples to carry out the ministry of caring in the Acts of the Apostles (6:1-3).

These men might best be described as helpers who took charge of the day to day care of those in need of food, clothes and basic money for household essentials. Scripture does not describe them as deacons. Their work bears only a slight resemblance to what we know as the ministry of a deacon. However, the term is used in the Deutero-Pauline Letter to Timothy and a description of the qualities necessary for the ministry is included:

Deacons likewise must be serious, not double-tongued, not addicted to much wine, not greedy for gain; they must hold the mystery of the faith with a clear conscience. And let them also be tested first; then if they prove themselves blameless let them serve as deacons. The women likewise must be serious, no slanderers, but temperate, faithful in all things. Let deacons be the husband of one wife, and let them manage their children and their households well; for those who serve well as deacons gain a good standing for themselves and also great confidence in the faith which is in Christ Jesus."

1 Tim 3:8-13

This is fairly reflective of how we think of deacons today. It includes the ministries of witness and proclamation and most probably included presiding at Eucharist. In our day the latter is restricted to presiding at Communion Services as opposed to presiding over the Consecration in the Mass. In our minds we rightly think of Phoebe fulfilling the qualities outlined above. Having the title and the qualities we can be certain that she exercised the role holistically. What a pity that as time went by men's emotional vulnerability became an issue, as did their need to be in total control at every level (1 Tim 2:7-12).

This whole area of diaconate and the current ministries involved therein has become one of great sensitivity in the Catholic Church in recent years. It is not a topic for public discussion but it is an issue deserving of reflection and prayer. The gentleness, sensitivity, creativity and empathy which women can offer in ministry and God's peoples' need for these virtues must never be overlooked or dispensed with. A faith community that dismisses the unique qualities that faith-filled women bring to holistic ministry risks depriving its members of distinct ingredients in what it means to be a truly Pentecostal or a Spirit-filled Eucharistic Community.

- How do you think women could help to develop a model of church that reflects more holistically the life-giving form exercised within the post Pentecostal community?

- How might local churches set about reviving the spirit of Pentecost?

Phoebe lived in a multi-cultural and multi-racial society. Like so many of her sisters and brothers in faith, she learned to inculturate both herself and the Gospel fruitfully. In Europe today we live in a constantly changing, expanding and struggling multi-cultural and multi-racial community.

- Can you think of ways in which you could:
  (a) do more to help diverse ethnic groups to communicate and become sources of enrichment in your area? and
  (b) offer helpful suggestions to your parish clergy, parish council, and even local bishop in relation to doing something about mutual inculturation, faith sharing and the enrichment of Sunday Liturgy?

- Should our churches be working together more closely in an effort to ensure that while immigrant families are supported in preserving their own traditions; they are also encouraged to engage with the local community in shared festivities with a view to ensuring that neither group feels a need to form protective ethnic enclaves?

False charges were brought against many in the early church as made clear in the case of Jesus and the wider discipleship. Many immigrant, and 'refugee women' coming into Europe today are women who have been carefully selected by drug barons and brought from third world or oppressed nations under the false premise that suitable useful employment awaits them on arrival. Illegal substances are planted in their luggage. They are accompanied by those who have deceived them. At airports in host countries they are pushed through Immigration Control, as innocent shields to their 'carers'; who are the main 'carriers'.

The innocent victims are arrested immediately while the real criminals walk free and stand to make large fortunes. This is a new way of 'bringing' false accusations before the courts. Unjust sentences are handed down by the judiciary. Prison chaplains struggle to support such victims; and labour in vain for justice, but their cries fall on deaf ears.

- Can you think of any effective way of highlighting or curbing this new form of 'false' imprisonment and persecution?

It is clear from greetings contained in the letter carried by Phoebe that women and men suffered greatly for their faith under Roman rule. Their story is repeated in many countries around the world today. According to figures issued by Aid to the Church in Need, there are two hundred and thirty million Christians suffering for their faith in over sixty countries in our day. Volunteers and members of Religious Orders are struggling daily in places such as Pakistan, India, El Salvador, Nigeria, Cuba, China, Haiti and Indonesia to name but a few countries where Muslim, Hindu, Sikh, and other extremists regularly target Christian mission, imprison or murder their evangelisers; pillage their properties and raise their buildings to the ground.

In an effort to suppress Gospel values, the greedy, power-mongers, fraudsters, and corrupt political dictators accuse missionaries and evangelisers who challenge them of causing riots, and of being revolutionaries and a threat to the state. These charges are as old as Christianity itself. They were brought against Jesus: *And they began to accuse him, saying, "We found this man perverting our nation, and forbidding us to give tribute to Caesar, and saying that he himself is Christ a king"* (Lk 23:2). Similar accusations were brought against some of their foremothers and forefathers such as Junia and Paul (Col 4:2-5).

As recently as 1980, missionaries Ita Ford, Maura Clarke, Dorothy Kazel and Jean Donovan learned the real cost of evangelisation when they were martyred in El Salvador. Like Phoebe, Junia and their co-workers these dedicated missionaries and evangelisers understood the demands of the Spiritual and Corporal Works of Mercy. They could have made the words of the late Archbishop Romero, their motto "Let us not forget: we are a pilgrim church, subject to misunderstanding, to persecution, but a church that walks serene because it bears the force of love."

Their sacrifices and prayers have contributed to some small improvements in El Salvador. However, the needy continue to be the victims of the greedy, not only in that country but in many other countries such as Zimbabwe, Darfur and Sudan. The faithful who seek liberation and justice through non-violent means continue to be treated as terrorists, revolutionaries and insurgents (Lk 23:10-16; Acts 17:5-7).

- Are there any ways in which you or your parish could highlight the plight of missionaries?

- What is the greatest obstacle to religious and social liberty in mission areas such as Chile, Zimbabwe, South Africa, Haiti and Peru in our day?

Prayer

Ever Creative and Generous God, you chose Phoebe for the ministry of evangelisation as a home missionary in Greece; and as Paul's delegate in bringing the fullness of your message to the church in Rome. We praise you for her openness to your Holy Spirit and for her selflessness in ministry.

We thank you for the encouragement which she brought to the struggling Christian communities in Rome; and for Paul's affirmation of Junia and all the other women who devoted themselves to the Gospel despite having to undergo the humiliation of oppression and imprisonment.

For blessing all these women with true sight to see the only road that leads to you, and with hearts so full of love that they held fast to the Good News despite unrelenting harshness and persecution, we praise you.

We pray for all those women and men who minister in the name of Jesus, today, in both our home and overseas missions. Sustain them with your love and enrich them with your grace that they, like Phoebe, Junia and their co-workers, may be faithful delegates and ambassadors in your on-going work of redemption.

We pray too, for ourselves and for all widows, married couples and single people who make unconditional commitments to witnessing to, and proclaiming the Good News in our own day. We remember especially the innocent women who are imprisoned because of the deception and greed of unjust political dictators, drug barons and those engaged in human trafficking. We make this prayer in the name of Jesus Christ who gave his life for the Salvation of all peoples. Amen.

NOTES

1 Joanne Turpin. *Twelve Apostolic Women.* St Anthony Messenger Press, Cincinnati, Ohio. 2004. p. 95.

2 Edited by Raymond E. Brown, SS., Joseph A Fitzmyer, SJ., & Roland E. Murphy, O.Cam. *The New Jerome Biblical Commentary.* Prentice Hall, Englewood Cliffs, New Jersey. 1990, 1968. p. 832. Support for the inclusion of chapter 16, is also offered by *The Collegeville Bible Commentary.* The Liturgical Press, Collegeville, Minnesota. 1992. p. 1098, and by Mary Getty Sullivan. *Women in the New Testament.* The Liturgical Press, Collegeville, Minnesota. 2001. p. 254.

3 Mary Anne Getty-Sullivan. *Women in the New Testament.* The Liturgical Press, Collegeville, Minnesota. 2001. p. 254.

4 Elizabeth A. Castelli. *Romans in Searching the Scriptures Vol 2.* Ed. Elizabeth Schüssler Fiorenza. Crossroads Publ., New York. 1994. pp. 277-78.

5 Mary Anne Getty-Sullivan. *Women in the New Testament.* The Liturgical Press, Collegeville, Minnesota. 2001. p. 256.

6 Ernst Käsemann. *Commentary on Romans.* Trans. Geoffrey W. Bromiley; Grand Rapids: Eerdmans. 1980. p. 411.

7 Elizabeth A. Castelli. *Romans in Searching the Scriptures Vol 2.* Ed. Elizabeth Schüssler Fiorenza. Crossroads Publ., New York. 1994. p. 280.

Conclusion

In some ways the New Testament and the women whose lives, priorities and vision we find there, seems an eternity away from us, our way of life, our values and vision today. However, once we settle down to reflecting analytically on their values, their aspirations and their relationships, we realise that at a basic level humanity has not changed much since 'the Garden of Eden'.

In all their searching for Jesus, finding him, claiming him as their Saviour and then going out to share their wisdom with others, only one of them lost her vision. They were Spirit-filled women. Each had her own story, her own frailties and her own giftedness. Each presented us with a unique challenge: Mary, the Mother of Jesus, was a woman of stamina, determination and fidelity. She had a timeless ability to inspire, to support and to love unconditionally. Mary, the Mother of John Mark, was so focused on Upper Room hospitality that she never missed an opportunity to break bread with a visitor; while Rhoda's excitability caused Peter's life to be endangered.

We have grieved with Sapphira who had such an insatiable need for human approval, acceptance, popularity and affirmation that in the end it destroyed her. We have empathised with Euodia and Syntyche whose incontrollable urge to evangelise, to catechise and to involve people in ministry was so great that their own relationship disintegrated. Had it not been for Paul's diplomacy, powers of discernment and quiet facilitating provision, it could have caused a schism in the Philippian church.

We have rejoiced with women such as the generous, skilful and much loved Dorcas; with Priscilla whose scholarship and ability to be respectful won the confidence of the famous Alexandrian scholar Apollos and enabled her to lead him, discretely, to see that Jesus of Nazareth was indeed the Promised Messiah and Saviour. We have reverenced missionaries such as Junia who suffered imprisonment for the sake of the Gospel and Phoebe, who though the first commissioned member of the early church to bring the Good News to Rome, knew when to withdraw and leave the local church to assimilate it under its own leadership and at its own pace.

As we journeyed through these chapters we found many parallels with our own times, values, relationships, search for wholeness, compassion, freedom, reconciliation and justice. We recognise that most of us in the new enlarged Europe, now live in a multicultural environment which is not too dissimilar in skewed values, insecurities, search for God, and need to succeed from that of Joppa, Ephesus, Cenchreae, and Rome. Hopefully our reflections and our prayers have helped us to see, as our foremothers in faith did, that true wholeness is the fruit of a listening heart, a discerning spirit and is only found in Jesus who is the Way the Truth and the Light.